The Not So Great
American Novel

A Memoir

7/17/14

Mary & Bill

Thank you!

[signature]

James E. Doucette, Sr.

The Not So Great American Novel
By James E. Doucette, Sr.
© 2015 by James E. Doucette, Sr.

All rights reserved. Use of any part of this publication, whether reproduced, transmitted in any form or by any means, electronic, mechanical, photocopying, recording, or otherwise, or stored in a retrieval system, without the prior consent of the publisher, is an infringement of copyright law and is forbidden.

THE HOLY BIBLE, NEW INTERNATIONAL VERSION®, NIV® Copyright © 1973, 1978, 1984, 2011 by Biblica, Inc.® Used by permission. All rights reserved worldwide.

These Scriptures are copyrighted by the Biblica, Inc.® and have been made available on the Internet for your personal use only. Any other use including, but not limited to, copying or reposting on the Internet is prohibited. These Scriptures may not be altered or modified in any form and must remain in their original context. These Scriptures may not be sold or otherwise offered for sale.

These Scriptures are not shareware and may not be duplicated.

"Scripture taken from the New King James Version®. Copyright © 1982 by Thomas Nelson, Inc. Used by permission. All rights reserved."

ISBN: 978-0-692-37720-8

Interior & Cover Design by: Fusion Creative Works, www.fusioncw.com
Editors: Mindy Sampson and Sarah Kortright

Published by

AlohaPublishing.com

First Printing
Printed in the United States of America

Randy Pyles asked me a key question about the book: "Why are you writing it?" To which I replied, "For my grandchildren."

To my children, grandchildren, and the generations to come.

Contents

Introduction: Getting the Monster Back on the Table   7

Chapter 1: Legacy   9
Chapter 2: Childhood Memories   13
Chapter 3: From Bingo, Maine, to Brooklyn, New York   21
Chapter 4: Early Years   27
Chapter 5: Uncle Hermie and Uncle Allie   43
Chapter 6: High School and Friendships   49
Chapter 7: The U.S. Navy   55
Chapter 8: College   69
Chapter 9: Bank of New York: 1962 – 1966   71
Chapter 10: Marriage and Fatherhood   75
Chapter 11: Television Communications Corporation (TVC) and Warner Communications   77
Chapter 12: Adelphia Communications: June 1973   91
Chapter 13: Return to New York   95
Chapter 14: Teleprompter   99
Chapter 15: Cablevision Industries   115
Chapter 16: Move to Texas   123
Chapter 17: Starting Out on My Own   127

Chapter 18: Cablevision of Texas III, Empire Communications, and High Plains Cablevision	147
Chapter 19: Diversification, The IRS, and Politics	163
Chapter 20: The End of Partnership With Cable Investments	169
Chapter 21: First National Bank of Lockney	177
Chapter 22: Time to Retire	185
Chapter 23: Ranching and Cowboys	189
Chapter 24: Herding and Gathering Cows	201
Chapter 25: Non-Business Activities	213
Chapter 26: Church Family	223
Chapter 27: Reflections	229
Chapter 28: What I Live For	233

Introduction

Getting the Monster Back on the Table

I began working on this story at the urging of my wife, Denise, as I recovered from cancer (a non-Hodgkin's lymphoma). The "cure" is chemotherapy and radiation; the treatment causes you to lose your hair, which I had very little of to begin with. The mornings after chemotherapy, I felt like I had walked through a spider web.

As treatments progressed, my memory became worse and worse. I discussed this with my doctor who informed me this was to be expected. It's almost as if I lost some of my memory with each strand of falling hair.

There are techniques to combat memory loss: you can do word games, read, and generally keep your mind active. I also built model ships (a hobby from my youth). As therapy, I wrote *The Not So Great American Novel*. There have been many great American novels, but this isn't one of them.

I stopped writing when the cancer treatments ended. The draft sat idle until the fall of 2013. Our niece, Sarah, visited us, and I discovered she does freelance proofreading. We discussed my novel and she consented to read it. I cringed at the thought of someone literate reading my work. Without her insightful comments, copious editing, and encouragement, I never would have completed this project. Sarah passed my manuscript to Jeri Hawkins—my honorary niece, a real author, who critiqued my writing and reawakened my desire to complete this project.

I asked Sarah if she understood Dr. Frankenstein's dilemma: "How do you get the monster back on the table?" She inspired me and has suffered through my many rewrites. With each rewrite, my memory improved; the therapy worked! The story that follows is my recollection of events, as well as I can remember.

Chapter 1

Legacy

What follows is a long letter to my grandchildren: Matthew, Jimmy, Brendan, Janey and hopefully those generations not yet born.

At a seminar on leadership, I was asked, "What are you most proud of?" I answered without hesitation, "My children." I'm certain the answer that was expected was some great moment in capitalism. My only real legacy is my children, just as you, my grandchildren, are your parents' legacy.

In the song, "What a Wonderful World," there's a line that talks about watching babies grow: "They'll learn much more than I'll ever know." This is so true; all of my children are better informed and educated than I am.

- My oldest son, James, graduated from the University of Buffalo and Cornell University where he graduated with honors.
- Bernard, my second son, attended Pace University, where he received both bachelor's and master's degrees with honors in the time it takes most people to complete one degree.

- My daughter, Marie, graduated from the Rhode Island School of Design, widely acknowledged as the best art school in the country.
- Patrick, my youngest son, attended Southern Methodist University and graduated *summa cum laude*.

The two oldest boys are at the top of their respective fields. James is a partner in McKinsey & Co., one of the most prestigious consulting firms in the world. Bernard was recruited as head accountant for Lord Abbett, one of the largest privately owned brokerage firms in the USA. In the field of publishing, prior to e-books, Marie designed numerous book covers; it is a thrill to see a book with a cover designed by her.

One of the things that always impressed me about our country is how we reach out to others. When the Peace Corps started in 1961, I remember thinking, *What a great idea. I wish I could do that.* Now I'm living this experience through my son, Patrick.

I've had many special moments in my life; none compare to watching my children being awarded their college degrees, thinking: "Not a bad legacy for a kid from Bedford-Stuyvesant, Brooklyn."

The next question at the seminar was, "What is the most important thing you need to have a successful career?" Again, without hesitation, I said, "My wife." I pointed out that for a woman, it would be her husband. Without the support of your spouse, your chance of a successful business career is severely limited. In the case of Denise and me, it's clear to me that without her support, encouragement, and help, my road would have been extremely rough. When we started the business in West Texas, I flopped around until she moved to

CHAPTER 1

Lockney and organized the office. The key to our success was our marketing program, which she also organized and implemented. It's speculative whether I would have been successful without her; however, I wouldn't want to take that chance. Denise had a good understanding of the cable industry, an immediate grasp of computer operations, and an intuitive understanding of marketing.

I'm sure the class did not appreciate my answers, but maybe upon reflection, they will.

Chapter 2

Childhood Memories

I had just resigned from Warner Cable and was visiting my Aunt Irene in Maine. I took my family to visit the cemetery in Waite, Maine, where my ancestors are buried. While I was showing my children the graves of their great-grandparents, a woman came up to us and said, "I see you've come home, Jimmy." I replied, "Nice to see you, Mrs. Tupper. How have you been?" She responded, "Fine, except Chick didn't winter well." The conversation continued with questions about my mother and aunts in New York. We discussed how a "newcomer" in town almost burned down his house as he had forgotten to turn off the roof heater this spring. (This is a coil of wire under the roof shingles to melt the snow and ice in winter.) Mrs. Tupper pointed out that he was from "away" (that's the term used for anyone not from Maine). After exchanging goodbyes, Diane (my wife at the time) asked me, "When was the last time you saw that woman?" I had to think before saying, "Well, probably twenty years." This confounded her. I will always be from Maine, while someone who moves into the state will always be from "away." A down-east joke illustrates this. At a funeral for a man of ninety, the conversation at the graveside went like this: "It's too bad old Tom passed away; he was almost one of us." Tom had moved from "away" to Maine when he was two years old.

Visiting with Mrs. Tupper brought back a flood of memories from my early years in Maine, but I'm getting ahead of myself. Let me start at the beginning.

I was born on June 13, 1940, in Providence, Rhode Island. I was named James, after my father. My middle name, Edward, is in honor of my uncle who died of a disease contracted in the Orient while serving with the U.S. Navy prior to World War II. While researching my family history, I came upon a picture of my Uncle Edward; his navy rate was machinist mate, the same rate I held in the navy. (I had no knowledge of his rate when I enlisted in the navy.) My father's side of the family descended from the French and English. My grandmother's maiden name was Rush. My Uncle Leo Doucette researched the Doucette (modern pronunciation: Doo-set) family and has traced our ancestors back to Nova Scotia, where our knowledge of our history ends. In Nova Scotia there is a town named Doucetteville. The Doucettes settled in Nova Scotia in the 1700s and were forced out by the British in 1755 (this expulsion is the theme of the poem *Evangeline* by Henry Wadsworth Longfellow). Some of our ancestors returned to Nova Scotia years later and some stayed in New England.

My Grandfather Doucette lived in Providence, Rhode Island. He had a distinctly Gallic face and spoke with a French accent. My father, his six brothers, and two sisters were all born in Providence. My grandfather was killed in 1939 by a drunk driver. I know very little of my Doucette grandmother other than she was from England.

CHAPTER 2

My mother's maiden name was Jones and her family lived in Maine. My Grandfather Jones was a farmer and logger. He would farm in the spring and summer and work in the woods during winter. He plowed his fields with horses (no modern John Deere tractor), and used the horses to drag logs in winter. He was a large, strong man and bald as an egg.

My Grandmother Jones' maiden name was Taylor, and her first name was Elizabeth, hence the original "Elizabeth Taylor." She had a slight build, fair skin, and a warm smile. I know some of the Jones' family history; they were farmers and loggers. My mother was proud of the fact that she could have been a member of the Daughters of the American Revolution. When Grandfather Jones visited New York in the late 1940s, he was shocked that we had to buy ice. His comment was, "By God, soon we'll be paying for water!" Wouldn't he be surprised today.

During the war, my Grandmother Doucette displayed a four-star flag in her window. It was a practice for families to display a pennant in their window to show that they had a child in the military; each star represented a son or daughter who served. I remember reading a newspaper article about the "Doucette Four Stars."

At the outbreak of WWII, my mother, sister, and I lived on my Grandparents Jones' farm on Bingo Road in Waite, Maine. The farm was one hundred acres: fifty acres of field and fifty acres of woods. It was on this farm they raised my mother and her nine brothers and sisters. We moved to Maine because my father had volunteered for the army at the onset of the war. There was no electricity on the farm, and we had to use an outhouse, as there was no indoor plumbing. I remember my grandmother churning butter on the porch or in the kitchen. A churn is a barrel-shaped container with a wooden-handled plunger (also called a dasher). The plunger fits in the hole and butter is created by pumping the handle up and down. The butter was far richer than anything you can buy today. The government today would probably outlaw the butter as unhealthy (full of fat), but it sure tasted great.

There were pens outside the barn where the pigs were kept. One of my chores was to "slop the pigs" (i.e., feed them), scrape all of the leftover food into a large bucket, mix in grain, dump it in their trough, and run like hell for the house. The pigs were mean and would bite. One day my grandfather butchered a pig. This was done by tying a rope around the pig's back legs and lifting it up with a pulley attached to the barn. The rope was tied to a horse's harness. The horse would hoist the pig and my grandfather would slit its throat. One of my thoughts was, *You'll never get another chance to bite me again.* This stands out in my mind because the horse stepped on my foot while he was hoisting the pig; maybe this was the pig's final revenge. Grandfather collected the blood and used it to make blood pudding. In his own words, "We use everything on the pig but the squeal."

My grandfather had a big German Shepherd dog named Ranger. That dog scared me, although he never gave me reason. He looked mean, but wasn't. The irony is that this pig, which seemed harmless, was actually mean, versus a mean-looking dog, which was actually harmless. An early life lesson: "Looks can be deceiving."

I remember the one-room schoolhouse my sister went to, which was up the hill from the farm. I've heard the expression that "people walked uphill to go to school" and in this case it was true. My sister went to the same school that my mother and all her sisters and brothers attended.

CHAPTER 2

A produce truck visited the farm each week selling canned goods, etc. For some reason I thought it would be fun to ride on the back of the truck. When we got to the top of the hill, I jumped off. The truck was going fairly fast, and, on second thought, I realized that this stunt wasn't so smart. I scraped my knee, but no one saw me. I never repeated it.

I remember the apple tree in front of the house. I thought this was the biggest tree in the world and enjoyed climbing it. Many years later, I visited the farm and noted that it was just an average-sized tree, but for a three- or four-year-old, it was massive.

Off in the woods was a hop shack. This is where wagon wheels were made. The shack was a wooden building, with clapboard sides and a cedar shake roof. It was quite old, dark, and gloomy, and appeared to have an ominous atmosphere to me and I enjoyed playing in it.

I know that it was very cold in the winter but that never made an impression on me. I do remember harvesting maple syrup. The trees were notched and a spigot was installed on the tree. The syrup would drain into a cup; the cups were poured into a large caldron and boiled. My grandfather would scoop a ladle full of hot maple syrup and throw it into the snow. This was quite a treat, and maybe the original "snow cone" came from just such an idea.

I enjoyed living in Maine and moving to New York was a shock. I went from living in the great outdoors to being confined to an asphalt jungle. It took me fifty years to get back on a farm.

THE NOT SO GREAT AMERICAN NOVEL

Elizabeth Taylor (Grandma Jones)

Me, Grandpa Jones, Mother, and Steven Berkowitz

CHAPTER 2

Mary Jane Rush (Grandma Doucette), Age 14

*Lucille, Grandpa Doucette,
James (My father), and Joseph, 1934.*

Chapter 3

From Bingo, Maine, to Brooklyn, New York

We moved to Brooklyn, New York, after WWII ended. I believe we moved to New York with the expectation of being with my father. We lived in an apartment house on the corner of Ralph Avenue and Monroe Street. It wasn't long before we moved to 786 Madison Street; roughly one block over and one block up from Monroe. My mother acquired a piano after we moved, I don't know how. I believe she expected my father to join us, as she did not play the piano and my father was a self-taught musician.

We moved our possessions in my baby carriage. What little furniture we had was moved in my uncle's fruit truck, and it didn't take long. The building was one of three buildings that shared a common backyard and basement. Our apartment was on the fourth floor. We lived in what was known as a "railroad flat"—you could stand in the kitchen and look through all the rooms to the windows facing the street. In the kitchen, we had an icebox (no refrigerator), a sink, gas stove, and a kitchen table with a checkered oilcloth. When we needed ice, my mother placed a sign in the street-facing window in the living room that read, "Ice." The iceman would chip off a block, roughly 18" × 18", and carry it up four flights of stairs for fifty cents.

As we did not have a washing machine, Mother would use a scrub board to wash our clothes, run them through hand-cranked rollers to remove the excess water, and hang the laundry on a clothesline that ran from a tall pole in the backyard to our kitchen window. I heard the neighbors say, "Mrs. Doucette hangs out the whitest sheets." Her hands were always red and chapped.

In the basement, each apartment had a large bin to use for storage. Some of the kids in the neighborhood and I would fashion spears out of broom handles and razor blades and hunt rats down there. Another source of entertainment was the dumbwaiter (a pulley system built into the hallway between the apartments for hoisting groceries). While one of us sat in the dumbwaiter, the others would hoist it up and down. We also played handball and other games: stoop ball, box ball, stick ball, etc. It amazes me today that kids need so much to occupy their time. With a ten-cent handball we created an infinite number of games. Sometimes we didn't need to spend the ten cents, as we would fish a ball out of the sewer. With a bag of marbles, we would entertain ourselves for hours.

On Madison Street, I began my education in gambling. It seemed that there was a blackjack or craps game going on all the time. We would play on the stoop of the apartment house or on the stoop of the peanut factory that was located on the corner. The peanut factory was another source of entertainment. We would scale the roof from our apartment building and play cops and robbers. Today, when I hear young people say they are bored, I'm amazed. My life was never boring.

CHAPTER 3

My thoughts about people who are bored is that they have it slightly skewed; they are not bored, *they are boring*.

I didn't know it at the time, but I was beginning a street life that could have led me down the wrong path. One of the fellows that hung out with us on the corner was Pete Donovan. Pete was involved in a robbery and killed a bank guard. For this crime, Pete got the electric chair. Life on the street lent itself to crime. A bunch of young people standing around bragging about doing some crime will talk themselves into committing it. I was a bit younger than Pete's crowd. To this day, I can see Mrs. Donovan walking down the street on the day Pete was executed. Mrs. Donovan was a short woman. As she walked down the street, the horror of Pete's death was heavy on her, hopelessness etched on her face. Had I been older, this could have been me. Pete was not the biggest guy or the toughest; he was just there at the wrong time.

The Peter Donovan case led to a famous lawsuit, because he was questioned for three days by the police before he was allowed to see an attorney. The robbery happened in 1961 and he was executed in 1963 or 1964. Pete's case was one of the events that contributed to the Miranda Rights ruling in 1966.

It pains me to see young people heading down the wrong path. At times, I look at a young person and see another Pete and think, *Someday there will be another Mrs. Donovan*. That experience certainly deterred me and many others from crime. Even so, I will never believe in capital punishment. Pete's life was taken before he had a chance of rehabilitation or redemption.

What dictated the direction of my life was our church, Our Lady of Good Council. The church was the center of my early years. On Wednesday afternoons we were released from school for religious instruction. I made my first Holy Communion and Confirmation there. One day at our religious instruction class, we were scheduled to receive our lesson on sexuality. The teacher of the class was a Franciscan brother. He wore the traditional Franciscan robe with the white rope around his waist. Picture this: an early-twenties celibate monk teaching a class full of street-wise boys about sex. He gave the lecture while twisting the rope and looking toward heaven for guidance, sweat running down his face. Most of our lessons were from the catechism and for this I'm forever grateful. This early exposure to Christian faith has stayed with me throughout my life.

A Boy Scout troop met at the church and I joined the troop. I can remember hiking to the Alpine Boy Scout Camp. We rode the subway trains to the George Washington Bridge, hiked over the bridge and up the Palisades Interstate to the camp. That was quite an experience. We thought the camp was in the wilderness. To this day I tell people of my achievement as a Boy Scout. I joke that I was the longest serving Tenderfoot in the Brooklyn Council. I don't know if this is true but it's a good story.

One event I will never forget during my years growing up in the 1950s in Brooklyn happened at the local grocery store. It was the practice of the local grocers to extend credit during the week, with the understanding that the bill would be settled on payday. This was truly living "payday to payday." All purchases during the week were recorded in "The Book." One day my mother asked me to go to the store with a list of needed groceries. I gave the list to the grocer; he threw it back at me and, in a loud voice so that everyone in the store would hear, said, "The book is closed to the Doucettes until last week's bill is paid!" I made an inner vow on that day that

CHAPTER 3

this would never happen to me again. I told my mother what happened and said I would never go in that store again. I guess she paid the bill. We began trading with the grocery store on the next block after that. The nobility of poverty is overstated.

Years later, I was going to surprise my wife Denise with a Lexus. I picked out a car from the showroom; the salesman asked me how I was going to pay for the car. I said, "I'll give you a check." His response was, *"Really."* What went through my mind was the vision of the grocer in Brooklyn. In as sheepish a voice as I could muster I said, "Maybe you should call the bank." He responded, "I will." His body language and demeanor said: *Now I'll expose this fraud.* When the salesman returned, I asked expectantly, "Is the check okay?" In a quiet, subdued fashion, he replied, "Yes." I knew exactly what the bank said: "Mr. Doucette owns the bank." I did this once and will never do it again, but it felt good.

The idea of "allowance" was unheard of when I was growing up. I earned spending money running errands for people, collecting deposit bottles and occasionally shining shoes on Broadway. The best corner to shine shoes was Broadway and Gates Avenue, but this was a hard corner to work as the bigger kids would run you off. I was earning money this way when I was eight, nine, and ten years old. This was typical of kids my age at that time. I always found a way to earn my own spending money. From this early experience, I began to realize that it is always possible to make money. I've heard people say, "I won't do that," as if this is below them. I believe that each person working to support his or her family, no matter the work, should be treated with respect.

The people living on Madison Street were of Irish and Italian descent. Many of the men were WWII vets and the women that worked, for the most part, were waitresses. My mother worked as a waitress for a number of years. Later, she got a job in the Adelphia Hospital as a practical nurse. This provided steady paychecks, but required her to work whatever shift the hospital assigned. The shifts varied and this is when my sister and I first learned to take care of ourselves. At that time, I was around seven years old. I remember one day when it was raining, I went to the bus stop and waited for my mother with our only umbrella. I think she really appreciated it.

Chapter 4

Early Years

My first day of school in 1945 was memorable. My mother dressed me in knickers! For young people today, this is not in their vocabulary. Knickers are loose-fitting short pants gathered at the knee. This type of pant was popular in the 1930s and was out of date by at least ten years or more. What possessed my mother to send me out dressed like that I'll never understand. Here I am with a funny accent, dressed like a child from a Dickens novel, going to school in Bedford-Stuyvesant, Brooklyn. This was not a good way to begin. The kids in my class had a great time making fun of me, thus began my lessons in fighting. Luckily, the knickers were soon replaced with second-hand clothes from our relatives. I can't say I enjoyed Public School (P.S.) 26 because I did not. I had a lot of trouble reading, and because of my mother's schedule, it was not possible to get any help at home. Once, I stayed home from school because I didn't have a pair of socks to wear. I was too embarrassed to go to school without socks. I had other pairs of socks but I could not find them. My teacher came to the house and asked why I had missed school. When I explained, my mother became really mad. I think I shamed her.

To the extent I had friends it was because of my family. The best friendships I had were with my cousins Benny Berkowitz and Bobby Keyes. During those early years in Brooklyn, we were the outsiders. At this point, I have to describe the culture of New York. I read once that New York is a series of small towns located next to each other. One town was Irish, the next Italian, the next Jewish, etc. Where we lived in Brooklyn, at that time, was predominantly Irish and some Italian. When an Irish and Italian married, it was called a "mixed" marriage. I had a Maine accent and my last name clearly was not Irish. Occasionally, someone would try to make it Italian and pronounce it "Douche-etty."

Benny, Bobby, and I played together each day. After school, we would go to Aunt Frieda's, Benny's mother's, house. They lived two blocks away and Bobby lived across the street from Benny. My Aunt Frieda lived on the bottom floor of a four-story house on Gates Avenue. Her mother-in-law owned the house. One year we decided to plant a garden in the backyard. We had great coaching from my aunt. She was brought up on a farm and knew how to plant vegetables. When we needed fertilizer, she instructed us to gather horse manure. At that time, vendors would sell fruits and vegetables off a horse-drawn wagon. Benny and I followed the wagon for hours collecting fertilizer (horse manure), scooping it up with a coal shovel into a fruit basket. I can remember how proud we were of the garden; it really did produce a lot of onions, cucumbers, and beans.

P.S. 26 was on Gates Avenue, just down the block from Aunt Frieda's house. Many afternoons Bobby, Benny and I just made it to the door with a gang after us. The desks at P.S. 26 sat double; you shared the desk with someone else. One

CHAPTER 4

year, when Bobby was told to sit next to a black boy, he stated, "I ain't sitting next to a n-gger." That afternoon the gang was rather large. Seeing that we were outnumbered, we ran like hell to my Aunt Frieda's house. The last scuffle was on her stoop where she interceded to save our lives. After that, Bobby sat where the teacher told him.

One year Benny and I decided that we would go hunting in upstate New York. At this time, we were around 15 years old and Benny had moved to the Flatbush section of New York. Benny already had his hunting license, but I still had to get one. At that time, I was working each day in a grocery store and could not make the hunting classes, so Benny took the class again using my name and secured a license for me. We went to Port Authority and took a bus to a town Benny knew of. He had friends that told him where to go and how to get there. By this time, Benny had bought a shotgun and borrowed one for me. We got to a field and split up to walk the field and flush a rabbit. Suddenly, a rabbit ran between us and Benny turned and began to blaze away. I hit the dirt! Luckily, we did not kill ourselves.

My Uncle George and Aunt Leola, Bobby's parents, and his siblings, Georgiana and Johnny moved in and out of New York depending on my Uncle George's latest bankruptcy. My Aunt Ruth married Herman (Hermie) Berkowitz when I was around eight years old. Their son, Peter, was born around 1950. When Pete was around three years old, Aunt Ruth decided to go back to work at Adelphia Hospital. She was a registered nurse. After school, I would baby-sit Peter until she got home. The money I earned allowed me to buy my first bicycle. I was really proud of it. It was a twenty-six-inch bike. As our bin in the basement was full, my friend Georgie suggested that I keep it in his basement. My bicycle did not last long; it was stolen. I believe that it was stolen by Georgie, one of my Madison Street "friends." So much for friendships in Bedford-Stuyvesant (Bed-Stuy).

It was typical on Saturday afternoon that we would all go to the movies. One day, the first 3-D movie was playing. On that particular day, Pete came with us. Benny and I thought it would be fun to sit Pete in the front row wearing his 3-D glasses. The first object that appeared to jump out of the screen sent Pete screaming out of the movie. When we got home, our parents were really mad. I've heard Pete tell of this many times, and even today he chuckles.

My father would show up to visit every year or so. One time he took me to a bar and played the piano. When he brought me home, he gave me a dollar. I showed the dollar to my mother. She exclaimed, "I work endlessly to earn money to support you, and he shows up and gives you a dollar and you think it's wonderful." This went on for a while. I finally went over to the gas stove, lit a burner, and burned the dollar. My mother said, "Why did you do that?" I said, "Now you don't have anything to complain about."

My dealings with my father were sporadic. He would show up after a year's absence as if nothing had happened. Usually he was drunk. He showed up at Christmas one year and knocked over the tree. To this day, I dread Christmas.

I do not know all the details, but my father ended up in New York. We had several conversations and he knew a lot about the Southwest. I believe he worked as a waiter in his travels. He had a variety of jobs: waiter, chef, piano player, etc. He was an alcoholic. I can't figure out how he did it, but he got a job in the New York City Morgue. One morning I

CHAPTER 4

went to meet him for breakfast and he introduced me to the "Head Man." When I asked if he was his boss, my father said, "No, when they do autopsies, it is this man's job to cut off the head." My father had a sense of humor.

I'm convinced that families can pass on substance abuse. On both sides of my family, we seem to have a disproportionate number of alcoholics and drug addicts. This finally registered with me many years later when Denise and I first moved to Lockney, Texas.

I can't recall why, but Denise had to visit her family in Florida. I was on my own. The first night she was away, I got home from work and proceeded to drink half a bottle of Jim Beam mixed with sweet vermouth (AKA, a Manhattan). The next day I started a little groggy but managed to get through the day. That night when I entered the house, my hand reached for the bourbon. Suddenly reality struck me, and I said to myself, *What the hell is wrong with you? Don't you remember your mother and father?* (For those reading this, a warning: if your family has a history of alcoholism, that problem is just under the surface and can emerge at any time.) I put the bourbon away. While I enjoy a glass of wine and have to admit that the Irish make good whiskey, I never drink alone or to excess.

I didn't learn much about my father until after his death. My Uncle Leo Doucette and I corresponded for a number of years prior to my uncle's death. In addition to telling me about my father, Uncle Leo also sent me information about the Doucette family.

As I said before, my father fought in WWII and received two Bronze Stars and three Purple Hearts. He fought at the very first battle in Tunisia at the Kasserine Pass, led by Major General Lloyd Fredendall, where he received his first Purple

Heart. I believe he was part of the Invasion of the Italian Peninsula at Anzio. He fought the length of Italy and entered Rome. He was in General Ridgeway's Honor Guard. My father never talked about his time in the war. I think the best resource to understand men like my father is represented in *The Greatest Generation* by Tom Brokaw. One thing I've always been grateful for is having known so many of these heroes. I don't think my father ever got over what he went through during the war. My Uncle Leo told me that my father was one of the most decorated soldiers in Rhode Island. Our nation was served well by men like my father. His service has provided me with a standard of patriotism I've tried to live up to, but also a lesson—the scars of war are long-lasting.

My parents never divorced despite never living in the same house for an extended period of time. My mother told me of their few early years together, but not any real details. Shortly before my mother died, she told me that she never loved any man like she loved my father. My father separately said exactly the same thing. I'll never understand their relationship or why they stayed married. Their New England unbending nature, I guess. Their lives could have been so much better. I vowed that my marriage would not be like theirs. We learn life's lessons not only from positive experiences, but unfortunately, we learn from tragic ones also.

At the time of my mother's death, she was visiting my family at our home in New City, New York. My Aunt Leola was living in Providence, Rhode Island. On a September morning in 1976, I left the house and drove to Rhode Island to pick up my aunt. It was a pleasant day and the trip was filled with the beautiful colors of southern New England. I picked my aunt up mid-day. We had a nice weekend planned

CHAPTER 4

and talked about the summers I had visited her in Maine. The drive passed quickly. This had been a much-anticipated trip, and we looked forward to spending time with my family and my mother. By this time, my life was on an upturn, having recently returned to New York from Pennsylvania, purchased a new home, and started a job at TelePrompTer Corporation. It was a joy to be with my aunt; she was always encouraging when others belittled me. Her life had not been easy, but she had found joy in the most difficult times.

We arrived at my house in the late afternoon. Upon entering the house, we were greeted by Diane's aunt, who exclaimed, "I know nothing – you must go to Nyack Hospital." She had been ushered to stay with my children as Diane had accompanied my mother to the hospital. Arriving at the hospital, Diane informed me my mother had had a heart attack. I was immediately presented to her attending physician, who informed me that my mother's condition was terminal as she had suffered a massive heart attack. This was beyond my comprehension.

I knew her spinal cord had partially disintegrated as the result of a fusion that had failed. She had retired, but was keeping herself busy working hospice patients. She would put on her brace and go help others. Once I said to her, "Mom, how can you do this?" Her reply was, "These people are really sick; all I do is limp a little." My mother was not one to be dissuaded once she made up her mind to do something.

I had one more visit with Mother. She was "nurse enough" to know her condition. Our final conversation is a blank. Without my Aunt Leola by my side, I don't know how I'd have been able to carry on. Many people arrived: my sister Marilyn, Fred (my mother's companion), my nephew Brian, and several others who I can't recall. After much turmoil, I arranged her funeral and burial. There are things that happen at a person's passing that should not be talked about. Times like these bring out the worst in people.

I'll share one thing. After the funeral, we went back to my mother's apartment. Several people were helping themselves to her meager possessions. I did not care what they took, except for one thing—I could not find her favorite poetry book. All I said to the assembly was, "I'm leaving the room, and when I return, the poetry book had better be on the table." After five minutes, I returned, and the poetry book was on the table. To this day, it's one of my treasured possessions, beer stains and all.

During the time my mother was laid out in the funeral home, my father visited to say goodbye to her. He had arranged with the funeral home for a private viewing.

My father became very ill with cirrhosis of the liver. I visited him in the Veterans home in Providence, Rhode Island, several times. He had retired from his job in Brooklyn and had moved to Providence to live with my Uncle Leo prior to becoming ill. My Aunt Lucille called me to tell me of my father's passing on October 22, 1984. He had prearranged the funeral. My sister Marilyn and I had to go to the Veterans hospital to pick up his clothing and personal effects—a difficult task. I blocked out most of what we did after that until we were at the graveside. As Father was a veteran, there was a small honor guard. I was presented with a folded American flag by a soldier, who said, "On behalf of the President of the United States and a grateful nation, I present you this flag for your father's service to this nation." My father was a hero and deserved this final tribute. I have this flag, his army medals, and an old clock he gave me when he moved away from New York. No words can describe

CHAPTER 4

the empty feeling at the loss of my parents. We have a merciful Lord and I'm sure they are finally together.

Most summers my sister and I were sent to visit our relatives in either Rhode Island or Maine. Usually a relative would drive us or Mother would take us. One summer, when Marilyn was around 11 years old and I was about eight years old, we went to Maine via the railroad. Each night at midnight a train left Grand Central Station called *The Excursion* (i.e., the Mail Train). This train stopped at every town from New York City to Boston. With each stop, the conductor would walk through the train and announce the next stop. The chairs on the train were made from rattan and stiff as boards. My mother put us on the train with a bag of sandwiches and a note. When we arrived in Boston, we were to find a policeman and show him the note. The note said, "We need to go to the North Station." A policeman found us a cab. When we arrived at the North Station, we gave the cab driver an envelope our mother had given us with a couple of dollars for the fare. Next, we had to find a conductor to direct us to the train to Bangor, Maine. When we arrived in Bangor at around 7:00 pm (approximately a nineteen-hour trip), our Uncle Paul Lowe met us. After a three-hour drive, we arrived in Princeton, Maine—our summer refuge from Bed-Stuy. Our cousins treated us well. They included us in all their activities and made us feel welcome. My Aunt Irene and Uncle Paul were warm, loving people. My uncle worked at the paper mill in Woodland. He had worked in all areas of papermaking, from floating logs to running the milling machinery. Their house in Princeton, having come from our apartment in Brooklyn, seemed like a mansion. We swam, fished and had a scoop of ice cream each night. The trip on *The Excursion* is one I will never forget.

I thought it was a great adventure. The sounds, smells and noises in my young mind were extraordinary. Our summers away from Brooklyn were the best of times.

As the neighborhood changed in Bedford-Stuyvesant from white to black, it transitioned from poor to ghetto. During the late 1940s and early '50s, people in Bed-Stuy had dreams and aspirations. As the neighborhood changed, there was no longer talk of moving out of the neighborhood and buying a house, or of kids finishing high school and working in a good trade or profession. Slowly optimism was replaced with a grinding, monotonous struggle to survive, reinforced by a dehumanizing welfare system.

As the last of the white folk, life was hard. I remember being surrounded by six or seven black boys and being pelted with snowballs. In the middle of this, one of my black friends jumped in. Thank God for Willy Simmons; he was a big kid and everyone was afraid of him. In a fair fight, I was able to give as good as I got, but without Willy that day, I would have been really beat up. Instead of being beaten until my attackers arms got tired, I only ended up with a black eye and a sore hand. By today's standards, it would be cause for calling lawyers and social services, but back then, it wasn't given more than a shrug by your mother. Fighting was a part of the culture.

The philosophy of Brooklyn at this time was to settle the slightest issue with your fists. I recall seeing two grown-ups fighting outside Moran's Bar, the place my mother spent her Friday and Saturday nights. They pounded on each other, and when they got tired, they would stop, drink some beer, and resume pounding on each other. It seemed like the entire neighborhood showed up. No one made any effort to stop the fight; this was the best show in town. These men were probably

CHAPTER 4

WWII veterans, and no one knew about post-traumatic stress syndrome (more commonly, PTSD). From these experiences, I developed a dislike of fighting. While the idea of standing up for your honor sounds very macho, the consequences can injure a person for life. I saw this in the navy. One guy stood up and punched another because of some slight. The fellow that was punched had split vision in his eye as a result, while the fellow that defended his honor has to carry this guilt for the rest of his life.

THE NOT SO GREAT AMERICAN NOVEL

Doucette Four Stars

CHAPTER 4

Madison Street, 2009, "Roughly Unchanged"

Mom and Dad (James and Eunice Doucette 1946-47)

THE NOT SO GREAT AMERICAN NOVEL

Marilyn, Mother and Me

Marilyn's Holy Communion

CHAPTER 4

My First Holy Communion

Chapter 5

Uncle Hermie and Uncle Allie

The people that formed a lasting and positive impression on me were my Jewish uncles – Hermie and Allie. They had married two of my mother's sisters and lived on Gates Avenue. I found out many years later that my Uncle Allie was never married to my Aunt Frieda. This will never diminish my feelings for Uncle Allie or make him seem any less of a real uncle to me. Hermie and Allie had a brother named Willy; I always called him Uncle. Their advice and counsel over the years has been invaluable. I've said to a number of people, if you don't have a Jewish uncle, adopt one.

Uncle Willy and Uncle Hermie owned a fruit store in downtown Brooklyn—Willy's Fruit Market. Uncle Hermie received ten thousand dollars in pay from the army and gave five thousand dollars to his mother. When the store was purchased, Hermie and Willy each contributed five thousand dollars. I did not know these details until after Uncle Hermie had passed away. I imagine that Willy got the money for his share from his mother. They worked together for over thirty years as equal partners. My cousin Peter Berkowitz and Willy's son, Barry, eventually inherited the store. They sold the property in the late 1990s for $1.4 million. I don't know if my uncles would have been proud or said, "You should have held out for one and a half." I'll find out when I join them in heaven.

I learned many valuable lessons from Uncle Hermie. He was about five foot five, and had a solid build. He was the strongest man I've ever met. He would throw a hundred-pound bag of potatoes at you with a flick of his wrist. He would take me with him to the fruit market on Sundays to help load his truck. My wage for the day was a dollar and lunch. He'd buy me the biggest sandwich I'd ever seen and an order of the best french fries I ever tasted. The days loading the truck were filled with good-natured jests and hard work. I looked forward to the trips. I don't remember him ever getting mad; he always had a sunny disposition. After what he had been through, he believed every day was a good day.

Uncle Hermie was in the army in WWII. Early in the war, he was captured by the Germans and spent more than two years in a POW camp. He never talked about it, but I've been able, over the years, to piece together a story that illustrates his experience. Several of the nephews worked with him at various times, and each picked up small details. The story I've gathered was that at the end of the war, as the Russians were approaching the prison camp, the German guards fled. Uncle Hermie reasoned that the Russians hated the Jews more than the Germans did. As related to me by my cousin Peter, Uncle Hermie decided that he would walk from Poland to the American lines in Germany. As he told it, he pushed an old baby carriage all the way and survived by eating whatever he could find in the ditch. When my cousin asked, "Why did you push a baby carriage?" he responded, "So I could stand up." I remember that each day he would eat a bowl of cereal

CHAPTER 5

with the same spoon he used in the prison camp. The spoon had an iron cross on it, the symbol of Nazi Germany. I don't think he ever said this, but it was from him that I came to this conclusion: you can either be a prisoner of the past or live for the future. Although any thoughtful person will think of the past and wish he had done things differently, it is pointless to dwell on it. My Uncle Hermie made it a practice, when he knew that times were tough for my mother, to bring us a sack full of fresh fruits and vegetables. I heard him say many times, "You've got to take care of your family."

Another example of how my uncles viewed helping out family happened when I graduated from Pace College. Uncle Willy asked me what I was going to do for a living. At that time, I was pretty well established in cable TV. Uncle Willy thought that I should get a Certified Public Accountant (CPA) license. He felt that as a CPA I would always make a living, and that it was a respected profession. I tried to explain that I was doing okay, and that if I wanted to be a CPA, I'd have to work for a CPA for two years, probably at a lower salary than what I was now making. His response was, "What do you need?" I said, "I'd need a letter from a CPA stating that I had worked for him for two years." He said, "You need a letter? I'll call my CPA, Morris, and he'll give you a letter. I pay that idiot a small fortune—he'll give you a letter." I finally persuaded him not to call Morris.

After my Uncle George's final bankruptcy in the mid-1960s, he and my Aunt Leola lived with my Uncle Hermie and Aunt Ruth. Uncle Hermie took them in when they did not have ten cents. The story goes that Uncle George picked up Aunt Leola one night after work and drove out of Maine with not much more than the clothes on their backs. After a number of years, Uncle George got a job and began to rebuild his life. Something came up between Uncle Hermie and him, and Uncle George called him a "dirty Jew." I'll never forget Uncle Hermie's response: "It's a stupid man that doesn't know who his friends are." There was not any anger in his voice; he was just stating the obvious. Uncle Hermie was the strongest man I've ever met, both physically and emotionally, and a very forgiving person.

Uncle Hermie had an intuitive business sense that I observed and benefited from. One year I sold Christmas trees and sold out early. Uncle Hermie also sold trees. I called him and asked if he had any trees I could buy from him. He asked, "Did you make money?" My response was, "Yes," so he said, "Shut your mouth, take your money, and go home." This says a lot: be thankful for what you got and don't be greedy.

The Mafia ran the central fruit market in Brooklyn. Every storeowner was obliged to buy from them. I know Uncle Hermie had to deal with them, but he never got too close to them. I heard him say many times, "If you lie down with dogs, you get up with fleas."

The Brooklyn Mafia was a tightly controlled organization made up of men of Italian descent – both parents had to be from Italy, no "crossbreeds." I remember one Italian shoeshine boy. He was industrious and you could tell from his dress that he was poor. One day he showed up in a new suit, driving a convertible car—he was a "made man." From that day forward, everyone stayed clear of him.

The Mafia controlled several businesses. Infringing on their business was dealt with harshly. A big business for the Mob was produce. At that time in Brooklyn, fruits and vegetables were often sold from a horse-drawn wagon. This business was

CHAPTER 5

controlled by Mike Torso. You rented the horse and wagon and purchased the produce from Mike. One fellow decided that he was not going to pay Mike and purchased his own horse and wagon and brought in his own produce. Soon after, the fellow was found dead; the wagon had run over his head and the horse was shot. I don't think anyone tried to freelance after that.

Another business controlled by the Mob was loan sharking. Typically, you borrowed ten dollars on Monday and would pay back fourteen dollars on Friday. If you did not pay the loan in full on Friday, you were expected to pay the "Vig" (i.e., vigorish) four dollars, with the understanding that by next Friday you would pay fourteen dollars. Failure to pay was unacceptable. The practice of kneecapping originated with this enterprise. If you failed to pay, your kneecap would be broken with a baseball bat, along with the admonishment, "Every time you limp, you'll remember to make your payments."

My uncles purchased their produce in the Brooklyn market, as did every other merchant. It was a well-organized business. My uncles' store on Smith and Pacific Street carried the widest variety of produce available in that area of downtown Brooklyn. When you looked at their stands, it was like looking at a work of art. Nothing was ever thrown on the display stands; the colors were balanced, with green, yellow, and orange produce breaking up arrangements. Every apple, tomato, and green bean was washed prior to being put out.

One day a local "made man" visited the store. I was not there, but the conversation went as follows:

"Willy, I hear that your son, Barry, is shylocking (lending money at extortionate rates of interest) to the Puerto Ricans."

Willy's response: "I did not know that."

Response: "We thought so. You have a nice store here."

With that, he walked out of the store. That ended Barry's shylocking business.

The uncles purchased the store next to the fruit market so that Uncle Allie could open a linoleum and carpet store. The story goes that they borrowed some of the money from Meyer Lansky, a Mob affiliate. None of the uncles walked with a limp; I guess they paid the money back.

Uncle Hermie, 1950s

Chapter 6

High School and Friendships

Attending P.S. 26 was not a great experience. When I was in my senior year, I remember a teacher telling the class to make sure we graduated "because it's probably the only diploma you'll ever get." *Talk about inspiration.*

I decided that the high school I wanted to go to was Chelsea Vocational High School in Manhattan located on 14th Street just up from Canal Street. I chose this school because I wanted to be an auto mechanic. The two years at Chelsea were the best school years of my young life. I remember getting off the train at Canal Street, where I had to walk across to Broadway and go up to 14th Street. It was never boring walking across Canal Street. World War II surplus stores lined the street with an ever-changing assortment of gear. It also bordered China Town. The stores sold WWII equipment, tents, knives, dud hand grenades, German rifles, and the like. To a young boy, this was about as fun as it gets.

The students of Chelsea High School came from all of the five New York City boroughs and were a diverse ethnic mix. It was a vocational high school with automotive, woodworking, and electrical programs. I got along well with most of the students and teachers, a first for me in New York. Since the school was so diverse, I was just another student who spoke a little differently. Many of the teachers were WWII veterans who were able to go to college because of their veterans benefits. They had a worldview far different from the non-veteran teachers I encountered later. I believe these men really cared about us and wanted us to be successful.

One of my best friends was Georgie LaBouy who was of Puerto Rican descent, born in New York and lived in Spanish Harlem. Harlem at that time had a large Puerto Rican population. I visited this area frequently with Georgie. Like Bed-Stuy, it was a poor neighborhood, but its character was totally different. When you got off the subway at 120th Street, it was like going to a foreign country; all of the store names were in Spanish. There was a market underneath the El Line, the largest market I had ever seen. You could buy anything from shoes to furniture, fresh fish, meat, fruits and vegetables—you name it. Each merchant had his own stand that varied from a simple table to a full-fledged store. The air had the smell of fresh produce and spice. It was full of activity and noise; all purchases were accompanied by reams of good-natured banter. It amazed me that anything could be accomplished in such confusion.

One time, George invited me to a "jump." When he first asked me, I had no idea what a "jump" was. This was the local name for a dance. It was at these jumps that I first learned to dance. We had great times dancing; it was at the beginning of the rock and roll era. We danced to popular music mixed in with Spanish music. The girls were friendly and taught me the dances.

I guess there were illegal drugs available but I never saw them. One of the boys at the jump was called Bembo. Many

CHAPTER 6

years later, I saw a television program about the drug problem in Harlem, and Bembo was featured in the program. This was not the guy I knew. It struck me how he had changed from a fun-loving person to a stoned-out drug addict. It was a tragedy and it could have been me. I hope that it was not Georgie's fate.

Once, Georgie invited me to his house for dinner. Mr. LaBouy was a short order cook in Manhattan. The apartment was neat and clean. At that time in New York, Puerto Ricans had a poor reputation. Many described them as "ignorant peasants who lived like animals." Much like all new immigrants, they were our generation's "them." Mr. LaBouy was a proud man and he had a dream. His dream was to return to Puerto Rico. He had purchased a new suit and shirts that he was saving for his return trip. It was something to hear him talk about his trip; he would return to his native land and let everyone know that he had done well in the United States. I hope that he was able to make his trip. One lesson I learned from this simple, decent man is that you've got to have a dream. I was aware of the racial prejudice the LaBouy family faced and felt honored to be accepted into their home.

A series of culture shocks seemed to mark my early years. My time at Chelsea began simultaneously as we moved out of Bed-Stuy. The area we moved to was known as the "Bushwick" section. It probably was not more than a mile from our place on Bed-Stuy. We moved from a predominantly black community to an Italian neighborhood. A person could live in this area and never have to speak English. The Italian neighborhood was also like a foreign country. This country was not anything like Spanish Harlem. The Italians seemed not to want anyone intruding on their world. As always, the Doucettes were foreigners. I made some friends in the area but none of these friends were long term. One day, I brought Georgie to visit and that was a mistake. I was told that people like "them" were not welcome in the neighborhood.

After my first year at Chelsea, I got a job at an Italian butcher store; it did not last long. One day the owner said, "Go home, boy." To this day, I have no idea what I did wrong. This was one of the first of many negative experiences I had as an employee. The next week, I started working in a delicatessen next door to the apartment house we lived in. Our apartment was over a liquor store. I suspect that my mother had something to do with me getting this job. She had informed me that she could not afford the expense of me going to high school and that I would have to pay my own way (lunch money and subway fare). It was around this time that a man moved in with us, Fred Sadoletti. When Fred moved in, it brought a stability that we had never had in our house. At that time, Fred was a bartender and would take horse-race bets for the local bookie. He was a decent and quiet man and always treated me well. I cannot say that I thought of him as my father because that would not be true. The impact on my mother was positive and I know he loved her. At seventeen, my sister Marilyn had a baby named Brian. Fred was there for my mother when she was forced to raise Brian. To Brian, he was Grandpa.

Working at the delicatessen was kind of fun, but it meant that there would be no more visits to Harlem and no more jumps. My workday was 3:30 pm to 7:00 pm Monday through Friday and all day Saturday, 8:00 am to 6:00 pm. For 27.5 hours a week, I was paid the grand sum of fifteen dollars. At that time, a loaf of bread cost twenty cents and potatoes were five cents a pound.

CHAPTER 6

At the end of my second year at Chelsea, my mother got it in her head that I should transfer to another school. This came about as a result of her conversations with a friend of hers, Joyce Becker, the idea being that I should go to a "good" school (in those days, that was New York code for *white*). They concocted a plan for me to go to Grover Cleveland High in the Ridgewood section. To do this, I had to have an address in that neighborhood, so Mrs. Becker put our name on her mailbox. Grover Cleveland was a "good" school, in a "good" neighborhood. My time at Grover Cleveland was marked with turmoil. Once more, I was the outsider. The Ridgewood section was predominantly German, same deal as the Italian neighborhood. One comment was: "What kind of a name is *Doucette*?" At the time, I had a vague awareness of my French roots.

Things at Cleveland started bad and stayed bad. On the very first day of class, a kid in my homeroom started a fight with me. I have no idea why. It wasn't much of a fight. He could not fight his way out of a paper bag. Many things have happened that I cannot explain and this is one of them.

This fight had a lasting effect. I walked into my Spanish class. The teacher took one look at my name and said, "You beat up my son and you will never pass this class." Her name was Mrs. Werhman (pronounced like *vermin*); she was true to her word. Apparently, the math and gym teachers were her friends and I ended up failing those courses as well. I'm one of the few people who can say he failed gym. I've always been happy that she did not have a friend in the cafeteria, as I probably would have failed lunch.

I was able to make these up in summer school. Luckily, I was also able to maintain my job at the deli. I'll never forget the civics teacher I had. He was one of those left-leaning liberals; New York at that time had many. He went into a lecture about how poorly the blacks had been treated in our country. I pointed out that, "If you were a white kid in a black neighborhood you'd really know what discrimination was." The next day, he dropped me from the class with a comment that "people like (me) should get a job with the sanitation department because that's all people like (me) were suited for." My English teacher had the class write about a typical day at school. After I turned the paper in, the principal contacted my mother. We had a meeting in his office and he had my mother read the paper. I described how the teachers treated me with open scorn and the hostility of my fellow students. I do not know what he was expecting, but my mother simply said, "If you don't want to know what he thinks, don't ask."

Me on the front stoop (High School Years)

Chapter 7

The U.S. Navy

On December 21, 1957, my senior year of high school, I joined the U.S. Naval Reserve. I was seventeen at the time and my mother had to give her permission for me to join. I was still in high school with the expectation that I'd graduate in June—which never happened. This enlistment program no longer exists; a high school student can enlist contingent upon graduation. That Easter holiday I went to boot camp at Great Lakes Training Center for two weeks. When the high-school year ended, I did not have sufficient course credits to graduate. I could have attended summer school and received my diploma, but my mother told me that I had to get a full-time job and pay my way, and that "four years of high school is enough." I got a messenger job in Manhattan, delivering mail and messages for R. H. Donnelly Company.

I reported for active duty at the Brooklyn Navy Yard on February 24, 1959, and was immediately assigned to kitchen duty as a mess cook. This lasted until I received my orders to report to the USS *William C. Lawe DD 763*, a destroyer in Newport, Rhode Island. Destroyers are referred to by sailors as the "greyhounds" of the fleet. The ship was built for speed with its hurricane bow and sleek lines. I served on the *Lawe* until February 22, 1961.

I was recalled to active duty in October of 1961 and reported aboard the USS *Remey DD 688* at the Brooklyn Navy Yard. Within one week, we were at sea. The U.S.S.R. was constructing the Berlin Wall; we believed war was imminent. Under my enlistment program, the navy could recall me to active duty. I was not too upset; my job at the time was not what I was looking for. The crew was made up of a small contingent of regular navy, reservists, and recalls. It was a strange mixture of people. In civilian life, for instance, the captain of the ship was a stockbroker and the first-class electrician was the captain's boss. The chief machinist mate was a florist. This was not your typical navy crew. Our first month at sea was, needless to say, a little nerve-racking.

The *Remey* was deployed to the North Atlantic. Our first port-of-call was Rotterdam, Holland. The dock was full of people cheering us. Our next port-of-call was Hamburg, Germany. As we sailed up the Elbe River, the ships in harbor saluted us with a blast of their ship's horn; again, crowds lined the pier. Both countries anticipated war and were happy to see the U.S. Navy.

In this chapter, the events cover my service on the USS *William C. Lawe* and the USS *Remey*. At times I've blended the stories.

Sea Duty

Sea duty with the navy was at times boring, thrilling, and terrifying. A watch can be filled with hours of monotony broken up by thirty seconds of sheer terror. During one cruise on the

CHAPTER 7

Remey, someone accidentally hit the collision alarm; all hands reported to their stations in record time.

A rough sea is beautiful—huge waves and white caps. You'll hear sailors describe it as "oily water." I was a mess cook during a storm on the *Lawe* (all enlisted men are required to serve three months working in the galley), and because of the rough seas, the only meal we could serve was a stew prepared in what is called a "gun boat," which is a deep serving pot. The stew was sloshing back and forth as the crew lined up to be served. Holding on with one hand, the sailors went down the "chow line" and we scooped a ladle of stew onto their tray. A number of sailors, with many years of sea duty, took one look at the sloshing stew and headed up the ladder, their green pallor was matched by the contents of their stomach as they held onto the ships rail. To all who returned, I'd offer an extra scoop as we had plenty.

Once I was standing throttle watch on the *Lawe* and the only way I could maintain my footing was to hold on with both hands. We had a gauge that measured the degree of list the ship took (the name of the device for measuring the degree of the roll). I asked the chief what degree of list the ship was designed for; he responded, "Just hold on, we've surpassed that many times." It was during this storm the USS *Essex* had her flight deck bent up (literally, curled). Our super structure support (half-inch steel) was so badly bent that it had to be cut away and replaced.

I served on the USS *Lawe* for approximately one and a half years. I studied and passed the test to be a petty officer. I had worked hard to understand the engine room. One of the proudest days I had in the navy was when my chief petty officer told me that on our next cruise, I would stand the top watch. Let me give a little explanation regarding engine room watch at sea. There were five people in each watch section (a four-hour shift). The watches were arranged around the clock starting when you got underway: for example, if you had the mid watch from midnight until 4:00 am, and if you were on a schedule (four on, eight off), then your next watch would be from noon until 4:00 pm.

The five watch standers each had a job. The throttle watch controlled the speed of the shaft; for example, if the captain asked that the ship cruise at one-third speed, the helmsman rang up (via the engine order telegraph) one-third and dialed the appropriate revolutions per minute (RPM). The throttleman opened a large valve increasing the steam flow to the turbines and brought the engine revolutions to the appropriate speed. The next watch stander was the lower-level man. He monitored the oil pump and all the pumps required to operate the turbines. The feed pump watch monitored and adjusted the feed pumps. These pumps fed condensed water back to the boilers. A messenger was assigned to take hourly readings on all equipment on the upper level, to wake up the next watch, and make coffee. The top watch was in charge of the watch standers.

I had been standing top watch for a number of months and really enjoyed it. The captain would have drills and put us through all of the possible problems that you could encounter. There were even competitive drills held within our squadron, which was comprised of seven destroyers. Impartial judges rated each ship's engineering department; the ship that scored the highest was awarded the engineering "E." The crew of the winning ship was allowed to wear a red "E" on the left sleeve of their uniforms. Our ship had won this and we all displayed our "E" with great pride.

CHAPTER 7

We were cruising in the North Atlantic while aboard the *Remey* and I was standing the mid watch. The engine room is a noisy place. After a while, you become used to it; most of us could hear the various pieces of equipment. A feed pump has a very specific whine, the oil pump sort of whistles, etc. We had a drill that required that we stop the shaft as quickly as possible, as a loud rumbling noise emanated from the reduction gear (the piece of equipment after the turbine). During the drill, the monitor would shout, "There's a loud rumbling noise in the reduction gear." The throttleman was required to stop the shaft as quickly as possible; this was a crucial test. We had performed well during our drills.

It was probably half way through the watch when I heard a loud rumble and ordered the shaft stopped. At this point, your training takes over. I ordered the throttleman to stop the turbine and ring up all-stop on the engine order telegraph; this informed the officer of the deck that the ship was coming to a stop he had not authorized. I got on the sound-powered telephone and informed the bridge that we had a loud rumbling noise in the reduction gear and I had ordered the shaft stopped. The other engine room had to follow, as to have only one shaft turning would cause the ship to go in circles; we were dead in the water.

Within a minute, the engine room chief and the engineering officer came sliding down the engine room ladder. The chief asked me what happened. I explained what I heard, and he said, "Okay, let's investigate." He had me disengage the locking gear that was secured when you stopped the shaft. As he talked to the captain on the bridge, he explained the situation and advised him what we needed to do. All of the watch standers were at their station. I was next to the chief, while he advised the captain that we were going to begin turning the shaft. In small increments, he ordered the engine speed increased. With each speed change, he and I listened and checked all the engine readings. He asked me, "Do you hear that noise now?" I responded, "No." We continued to increase speed until we had reached the speed we were at prior to the shutdown. The chief and the engineering officer stayed in the engine room another fifteen minutes. Finally, he asked, "How does it sound?" I responded, "It sounds fine." With that, the chief and engineering officer headed for the ladder and the chief said, "It's your watch. If there are any other problems, call me."

The incident was never mentioned again and I stood my normal watches throughout the cruise. No one questioned my judgment; they supported my actions without question. If you are able to develop an organization that has that much confidence and trust in its people, there are no limits to what you can achieve.

When a ship leaves port, all hands not on watch "man the rail." We lined up, evenly spread around the ship. Going to sea the first time was a thrill for me. I love the beautiful sunrises and sunsets in West Texas, they remind me of the sea. The United States Navy is today the unchallenged master of the sea. Let's hope it stays that way.

Shore Patrol

One duty that most petty officers had to do was shore patrol. When a ship was in port, they had to be responsible for their crew. The shore patrol acted as a "volunteer" police force that augmented the sailors assigned to permanent shore patrol in

CHAPTER 7

that port. The first time I was selected for this, I felt really honored. The honor quickly faded once when the USS *Remey* docked in Gibraltar. My chief approached me with the arm band and night club and said with a big smile on his face, "Doucette, you got the stick (our description of shore patrol)." I asked, "Ok, Chief, why the big smile?" He responded, "A transport full of British Marines just docked for a liberty call. Have fun." What went through my mind was a bar full of "bottle courage sailors" fighting with British Marines and the bar owner running into the street screaming "Shore Patrol!" and I would be required to separate the combatants, at which point I'd surely be killed. Luckily, this never happened. I ended up patrolling with the British M.P.'s. The British military was well disciplined. The men I patrolled with informed me what the Marines were told, "If you strike one U.S. sailor, you'll grow old in the brig (the ship's prison). Our crew and the Marines had a good time together and ended up swapping hats after a night of good-natured banter.

Another time I had shore patrol was in Charleston, South Carolina. The *Lawe* was in the yards for repairs. The enlisted men's club (the beer hall) was located outside the base. Another fellow and I were on patrol and our area covered the beer hall. Late during the patrol, the civilian manager of the beer hall chased us down, "Shore Patrol come fast! There's a riot in the beer hall!" My companion immediately pulled out his stick and said, "Let's go." Placing a hand on his shoulder I said, "Let's call for back-up. There are a hundred drunks in there; I don't feel like being clubbed to death by my own night stick." Good sense prevailed and with ten other shore patrollers, we separated the fighters and arrested the combatants. It took three men to wrestle one huge boatswain's mate to the ground. He ended up with a broken leg. My partner thanked me later for calling for back-up.

Shore Leave

The U.S. Navy had a policy of allowing us to purchase five bottles of liquor, once the ship had passed the three-mile limit. Picture this scene: young sailors ages 18 to 21 going on a weekend pass each with five bottles of whiskey—a formula for success. It was after one such weekend that I, and several of my shipmates, woke up in the Shore Patrol Brig; we were picked up for public intoxication. Looking through the bars, I could see my navy career flying away. The ship was leaving port that day and missing movement for any reason was a court-martial offense and possibly a less-than-honorable discharge. The chief petty officer in charge of the brig got us "sad sacks" in front of him. He said, "I know your ship is leaving today. I'm going to open the door and all I want to see are a--holes and elbows running to your ship." The brig was about one mile from the ship; I think we broke the four-minute mile. For this, we received one month's extra duty chipping paint, fighting the peace-time enemies, "rust and corrosion." I vowed never to repeat this.

I had been in Gibraltar a number of times. During one visit, a friend of mine, Sam Ebertshauser and I went on liberty together. We stopped at a local bar/restaurant for some drinks and snacks. For a reason only he knew, the waiter was extremely rude. I had to visit the restroom and noticed that a window faced an air shaft. When I returned to the table, I told Sam of my discovery. After some discussion, we decided we'd get even with the waiter and climb up the air shaft and stick the waiter

CHAPTER 7

with the bill. The ascent was easy. As we walked the roofs looking for a way to get down, we stepped on what looked like a roof but turned out to be a patio covering. We fell through to a courtyard full of people. Racing as fast as we could, we exited the courtyard. After this adventure, we decided it was time to return to the ship.

The next day, the engine room crew was gathered by our first-class petty officer, Don Acosta. He exclaimed, "Tomorrow the entire ship's company is going to be lined up for review by local residents." He continued, "I can't believe it, two animals crashed through their roof last night." I looked at Sam, and we said in tandem, "It was us." I'd rarely heard Don curse before and was amazed by his proficiency with expletives. We were called to the chief's quarters where the chief added several expletives I'd never heard. Later that day, we received our orders, "You will buy a bouquet of flowers and a box of chocolates and accompany the chief to the house you fell into the other night." We arrived behind the chief bearing our gifts. The entire family was there. The lady of the house immediately began to laugh, "You two look like my son who is in the military." They graciously accepted our gifts. We offered to pay for the roofing, which they declined. I thought, *What nice people*. They even served us coffee and cake.

After we returned to the ship, we were restricted to the ship for thirty days with extra duty. Sam and I spent many hours chipping paint during our free time. We were fortunate that nothing else happened to us. Our assistant engineering officer, John Lynch, asked us why we had done this. When we explained, he immediately exclaimed, "You did all this to get out of a bar bill?" I explained, "Mr. Lynch, it seemed like a good idea at the time." To this he just laughed.

Discrimination (Pre-Civil Rights)

Years after I got out of the navy, I read Colin Powell's biography; he grew up in Harlem and attended City College of New York. He wrote that he'd never witnessed racism until he went into the military. After the USS *Lawe* changed home ports from Newport, Rhode Island, to Jacksonville, Florida, I met a girl at a USO dance and she invited me to her house. I went with her and her family to a Southern Baptist Church. The Minister's sermon was about the "N-ggers, Spics, Jews and Cat-lics" and how they were "ruining the country." I was hoping he would get to the short list—the people he liked. After the service, I met the minister at the door. He asked if I was a "n-gger-loving Yankee." I was speechless. Being brought up in New York exposed me to a variety of people, many having prejudices focused on a group or religion. This was the first time I'd met a person with such a wide range of hates. I think I've coined a new phrase, this Southern Baptist minister was "an equal-opportunity bigot." (Remember where you heard this first.) This was my warm welcome to the South. Needless to say, I never went back to that church.

The reaction of the crewmen from the North toward racism was silent acceptance, and in some cases outright agreement. I remember one particular occasion when we spoke out. It was a custom that when we were going on liberty, we would pool our money and take a cab to town. This was not a formal thing. When four of us were standing at the gate, we would share whatever cab waited there, ride to the center of town and go our separate ways. One day at the gate, four of us decided to take a cab as usual. One of the crewmen was black; a second-class petty officer who we called Mr. Lloyd. Mr. Lloyd was a

CHAPTER 7

cook; he had served in WWII. His chest was full of ribbons with battle stars. Everyone called him Mr. Lloyd, even the officers. His general quarter's station (when the ship is preparing to fight) was gun captain. This station was normally held by a higher rank, but as Mr. Lloyd had this position during the war, it was natural for him to be gun captain. All of the crew looked up to Mr. Lloyd.

At the gate, three of us saw Mr. Lloyd and said, "Let's take a cab." We walked over to the cab and started to get in. The cab driver said, "I can't take him," referring to Mr. Lloyd. I'm not sure who said it, but it was what we all thought—"You're going to take us all to town." I said, "This man fought for you and you will not turn him away (*expletives deleted*)." The cab driver (who was visibly frightened) said, "Beat me up if you want, but if the Klan sees him in the cab, they'll kill me." Mr. Lloyd said, "Forget it, fellas," and walked away. One of the things the navy was noted for was that you always stand by a shipmate. This experience made a lasting impression on me. One of my minor protests, to the horror of the local rednecks, was to use the "colored" restroom.

Change of Plans

The navy was a positive experience. I worked in the engine room and really liked my job. My Uncle George had been in the merchant marines and also worked in the engine room. By this time, Uncle George had settled in New York and worked in a power plant. When I was home on leave, we discussed my future. He told me to learn all I could and he would get me in the union, and I could make good money working at a power plant. I studied hard and made petty officer. Things looked great. Upon separation from two years of duty on the *Lawe*, Uncle George and I went to the union hall so that I could join the union. We were informed that the union only accepted sons of members. Wow. What a setback. I had no idea what I was going to do. I read an advertisement for Adelphia Business School, which provided training in the operation of IBM electronic cardpunch machinery (pre-computer). It cost about five hundred dollars to attend the two-month course and they guaranteed job placement. When I completed the course, an interview was arranged with the Brooklyn Board of Elections (BOE) and I got the job. I worked at the BOE for six months.

Completing High School

During the time between serving on the *Lawe* and being recalled to serve on the *Remey*, I attended Fort Green Evening High School. I needed to pass algebra and English to get my high school diploma. I owe completion of the algebra course to my teacher. He was ex-military, and through conversation, he knew I had just gotten out of the navy. I was one of the older students in the class. I worked hard and was struggling, and my teacher knew it. One night, he asked me to stay after class; the problem we worked on that night was difficult and the class was leaving me behind. He wrote the problem on the board. While he watched, I tried to work the proof. After about ten minutes he said, "You have two sides to this equation—as you work through the problem, both sides have to stay in balance. What you need to do is play around with it." I finally got it. Without that tutorial I would never have passed. To pass the English course, I summarized all of the grammar rules I needed to know on one piece of paper and each day I

CHAPTER 7

read them until I had them memorized. I passed both courses and received my high school diploma, and concluded I would never teach mathematics or English.

Me in front of the USS Remey
(Rotterdam, Holland, December, 24, 1961)

Chapter 8

College

When I was nearing the end of my tour on the *Remey*, one of the officers asked me what I was going to do when I got out of the navy. His name was Mr. Tubesing. He was a good man. He treated the enlisted men with respect. I knew I did not want to go back to the BOE, but beyond that, I had no idea. Mr. Tubesing suggested I go to college. I said, "You've got to be kidding. People like me don't go to college." He responded, "Nonsense, look at what you've achieved in the navy." He explained how he had come from a poor family, was the first college graduate in his family, and had to work to pay his way through college. We even discussed his college wardrobe. "One sport coat with various combinations of ties, shirts, and slacks can be mixed and matched to be properly dressed for any occasion." This may seem trivial today, but at that time, it was expected that you dress appropriately for each occasion. While at sea, I would spend my free time reading. It was our practice to exchange books. He said, "I know what type of books you read. If you can read those books, you can go to college." With that, I sent away to City College New York (CCNY) for an admissions application, completed and submitted it. To my surprise, I was accepted; Ensign Tubesing was not surprised. He was one of the few people who believed in me.

As a condition of acceptance, I was required to take two non-credit courses: review English and review math—the same courses required to graduate high school. I began taking courses at CCNY in September 1962. After completing the review courses, I was able to attend on one condition. I had to prove that I could pass college-level courses before being allowed to matriculate for a degree. Thus began my college career.

Chapter 9

Bank of New York: 1962-1966

Upon separation from the navy, I applied to and was hired by the Bank of New York as an IBM machine operator. After one year, I transferred to the accounting department. The Bank of New York was a good employer. They provided a free lunch and had an employee lounge. I spent many lunch hours doing homework in the lounge. The bank encouraged its employees to go to college. The lounge looked like a school library.

The atmosphere of the Bank of New York's accounting department was a page out of a Dickens novel: the general ledger was prepared by hand using a fountain pen. Each night one person had to stay to post the ledger, a duty that rotated among five of us. The head accountant, Mr. Schneff, would set up the schedule so that the night students could take their classes. Usually, the posting and proof was completed by 10:00 pm, but this did not always happen. It was the clerk's responsibility to have the ledger in proof before 11:00 am the next day, when the Federal Reserve report had to be filed. I can remember staying to two or three in the morning and rushing home for a couple of hours of sleep. I would be back at my desk by 8:00 am looking for an error ('difference' in ledger language).

Each account on the ledger was the responsibility of a clerk in the department. The clerks responsible for accounts would take the posting tickets and update the detailed ledger. After this was complete, the posting clerk had to reconcile with the ledger. One individual stood out. He was originally from China and used an abacus to do addition and subtraction. He was the fastest accounting clerk in the bank and he would have his posting done before all others. After working almost around the clock, and the deadline for the Fed approaching, Mr. Yen would ask, "What you got?" I told him the balances shown on the ledger for his accounts; as he turned away, he said, "Wrong."

He really was a decent person, and although his communication was abrupt and somewhat cryptic, he was not malicious. This department was a disciplined operation. You didn't use pencil, you used pen. It had to be perfect. These methods are archaic today, but it taught me not to quit, and to stick to a task until you are complete.

I can still hear the infernal clicking of Mr. Yen's abacus (a wooden counting tool using columns of beads) as I pulled my hair out looking for my error.

I enjoyed attending CCNY, but at the rate I was able to take courses, it would take ten years to complete a degree. I transferred to Pace College during the summer of 1963 and completed the requirements by the fall of 1967. I became friendly with John Corbett (my future wife's brother). We talked about night school (he was attending Fordham Law School), and I told him how hard I had to study because I was a poor reader. (I didn't know it at the time, but I was struggling with mild dyslexia. I didn't realize this until I was in my late forties, when my son Patrick was in grammar school. I heard about it and

CHAPTER 9

thought...*that sounds familiar!*) John related that he had difficulty reading but had purchased a self-taught speed-reading course, and since he had completed the course, gave it to me. It took a few months to complete the lessons; I know I never would have been able to finish college without this valuable skill. I've recommended to a number of young people planning to attend college that they increase their reading speed and comprehension. During four years at Pace, I completed 121 credit hours, roughly 37 hours per year. Thinking back, I can't believe I did it working a full-time job and getting less than five hours of sleep each night. Time was a blur.

One course that I remember well was philosophy, taught by Professor Pollock. He made it known on the first day of class that he did not support the Vietnam War. Once he learned that I was a veteran, he went out of his way to ridicule serving in the military. I did not disagree with much of what he said, but could not abide his comments about those serving. He never asked, but had he, I would have explained my feelings.

The justification for the war was that a North Vietnamese torpedo boat had attacked a US destroyer (USS *Maddox DD 731*) in the gulf of Tonkin. At the time of this report, my reaction was, *This must be a joke,* as the *Maddox* was a sister ship of the USS *Lawe DD 763,* which I had served on. With the radar and armament of the *Maddox* it is doubtful that the torpedo boat could have gotten close enough to launch its torpedoes. This incident led to Congress passing the Gulf of Tonkin Resolution, which became Lyndon Johnson's authority to wage the Vietnam War. This was not a declaration of war as called for under our Constitution, and killed 58,220 of our soldiers all based on an incident that years later was acknowledged never to have happened. It bothers me that we as a nation have been involved with so many wars without debate by our Congress as required by the US Constitution. The precedent for the Gulf of Tonkin Resolution was the Korean War that President Truman waged without a war declaration, as it was a police action, which killed 54,229 US soldiers. These two non-declared wars were the justification for Congress not declaring war in Afghanistan, Iraq, Grenada, Somalia, etc.

I'm pleased that our country now welcomes our service members home lovingly. Those who served in Vietnam deserved the same treatment. Unfortunately, the Professor Pollocks of the world did not see it that way, but he never bothered to ask (he probably did not want to hear from "people like me"). It is wrong that our Congress does not exert its constitutional authority regarding war and has abdicated its responsibility to successive Presidents. I want our Congress to debate long and hard before our soldiers are sent to be killed.

Chapter 10

Marriage and Fatherhood

In February 1964, I married Diane Corbett and rented an apartment in the Bronx, not far from her parents. When James, our first son, was born on July 21, 1965, health insurance did not cover births, as it was considered self-inflicted (the policy's words, not mine). The total cost of the birth, including doctors and hospital stay, was six hundred dollars. It took us two years to pay for it. The night Diane's water broke, we took a taxi to the hospital. After getting her checked in, I was informed in no uncertain terms that I was not to wait at the hospital, and that they would call me. The next morning, I was awoken by a telephone call from my in-laws informing me that my wife had delivered a baby boy. I rushed to the hospital. Diane was less than enthusiastic, as she expected I would stay with her. I had no idea what was expected of husbands and fathers as I was never around one. Nonetheless, I was delighted. I called Mr. Schneff; he congratulated me and said I did not have to be in to work until noon. (Historic note: there was no "Family and Medical Leave Act.") My son's early years for me were extremely busy working and trying to finish school, but we had many wonderful days pushing him around in his baby carriage. He was a happy baby. I can see him now, pushing plastic bowls down the hall with such excitement, it still brings a smile.

One day, when I came home from school, Diane was in tears. She had found a cockroach on James and informed me that she wanted to move immediately. We moved to a New York City housing project in Queens shortly after this. My son Bernard was born on December 4, 1968, and daughter Marie was born on December 17, 1969.

On December 4, 1968, I received a call that Diane was going to the hospital. By the time I arrived, my father-in-law was already there. He informed me that I had another son. I said to him, "Let's go see little Bernard," (Bernard was my father-in-law's name) and I think I surprised him. Bernard, and the following December my daughter, Marie, were each born in Bethany Deaconess Hospital, where my Aunt Leola was the nurse in charge of the pediatric ward. What a joy it was to see her beaming, as she held up my newborn children. I loved my Aunt Leola. She was a gentle soul who I grew to know in my youth during many summers in Maine.

We lived in a two-bedroom apartment with a living room and a wide hall that we used as a kitchen. At night and on the weekends I'd do my homework at the kitchen table. We lived close, James running around in baseball uniform pajamas pretending to be a New York Met, Bernard in his high chair, his face full of cake, and me, holding Marie on my lap. Ironically, though we were struggling financially and lived simply, this was one of our happier times.

Chapter 11

Television Communications Corporation (TVC) and Warner Communications

After leaving the Bank of New York in 1966 (I worked at Bankers Trust for a short time), I accepted a job with Vikoa Construction Corporation as a contract administrator, my first job in cable television. The owner of the company was Arthur Baum. I reported to the general manager through a man named Mike Joyce, who reported to the owner's son, Bobby Baum. I would describe him as a typical spoiled kid and extremely rude.

Reporting to Mike Joyce was a trial, as he was an alcoholic. Frankly, I had no background in contract administration and Mike was no help. I was fired from Vikoa within a year. The fact that I was fired did not bother me, it was the manner. I remember being at my desk one morning, when the controller came through the office, made a joke to a fellow co-worker, and gave me a sidelong glance. Shortly after that, the personnel manager called me to his office, told me that I was being terminated, and that I would not receive any severance pay. Apparently, this firing had been planned by Bobby and the controller while Mike Joyce was out of town. I was to immediately leave the building. The fact that I was fired did not really upset me; I was a mismatch for the job and the company did not provide training. What upset me was the lack of human consideration. I went home and told my wife what had happened and thought it would be a good time to take a vacation and visit my relatives in Maine. Within one week of returning from vacation, I secured a job with Metromedia Music Company.

I worked for Metromedia Music Company for one year as a "business manager" (i.e., a glorified bookkeeper—I don't like title inflation). It was a music publishing company originally owned by Tommy Valando. The most notable thing about this job was that Mr. Valando was the publisher of *Fiddler on the Roof* and *Cabaret*. During this year, Diane and I attended several Broadway plays. One play was *Maggie Flynn* starring Shirley Jones and Jack Cassidy. I really liked the show, but it only lasted for two weeks.

One day while walking in midtown Manhattan, I met Jack Gault, a Vikoa vice president. After a short conversation, he arranged an interview for me with Gordon Fuqua, Executive Vice President of Television Communications Corporation (TVC), as he felt that I had not been treated well by Vikoa. I knew the people at Metromedia were not happy with me, as I did not fit in with the showbiz types. The day I told them I was leaving, they were relieved.

At TVC, I was the director of finance. Being fired by Vikoa turned out to be a good reference. This was my first exposure to having a position rather than a job. The position came with a private office, a secretary, and a defined area of responsibility. I don't understand what Gordon saw in me but I'm eternally thankful for his trust and confidence in me.

CHAPTER 11

It was my responsibility to do financial analysis of new projects, evaluate new acquisitions, and prepare the annual budget. In addition, I had to represent the company in front of the city councils when the company wanted to increase its monthly subscription rates. This meant I had to address a large audience and advocate the company's case for a rate increase. Gordon knew I was extremely uncomfortable speaking in public. (Side note: one course I almost failed in college was speech.) I could sit with him and present complex financials issues, but when I had to stand up and do the same presentation in front of a group, I would fall apart. Prior to my first city council meeting, Gordon talked about what I had to do and said, "Jim, you have got to get over this irrational fear of public speaking. The key is preparation." This was excellent advice. I presented the case and the company was granted the rate increase.

About a year after I started working at TVC, the company received the franchise to install a cable television system in Akron, Ohio. This was such a large project that we sent out bid sheets to suppliers for the equipment to be used. The bidder had to prepare detailed specifications and price quotes for the equipment. Each bidder was scheduled a meeting day to present their proposal. The day arrived for Vikoa's presentation. The format was that Gordon would meet with the bidders and then summon me to go over the proposal in depth. I had no foreknowledge that Vikoa was a bidder.

When I walked into Gordon's office, he introduced me to the people from Vikoa. The lead person from Vikoa was Robert Baum. I'll never forget Robert's face; he looked like he had seen a ghost. On the way out, he tried to explain that there had been a mix-up when I was terminated. I said, "Don't worry about it, things happen." (This was before Forrest Gump's "sh—happens.") With Gordon's permission, I threw the Vikoa proposal in the garbage. As they say, "Be careful of who you step on while you climb the ladder of success, as you might pass them on the way down."

I had several encounters with Robert Baum subsequently. He paid for his shabby treatment of me many times over. Years later, I heard that after Vikoa went bankrupt, Robert ended up producing porn films—a fitting reward.

Throughout my career, I had to terminate many people. I realized that this was, in some cases, the result of poor management or a change in the business that the employee had no control over. People who are mismatched for their job are put there by management. An employer bears the responsibility to correct its employment errors as humanely as possible. A person that is not competent at their current task doesn't mean they are incompetent for all tasks. I've helped many terminated employees find their next job. People in our society are proud of their work. Realize that the next thing you know about a person, after you know their name, is what they work at. Most people take pride in their work and it is one of the building blocks of their identity. When you terminate someone, you are destroying part of his or her life. I have read that after the loss of a spouse, the next leading cause of suicide is the loss of a job.

Union representation of workers was not widespread in the cable television industry. At the time I joined TVC, only one unit of three workers was represented by a union. The International Brotherhood of Electrical Workers (IBEW) represented the technicians who worked in the cable system serving Warren, Pennsylvania. As I was the junior member of

CHAPTER 11

the staff, Gordon informed me that it was my responsibility to handle union negotiations. He felt that this would be good experience for me. As part of my preparation for this assignment, I attended a two-week course in labor relations given by the American Management Association (AMA).

The contract for the workers in Warren was due to expire, and I had to negotiate a new agreement. Gordon and I discussed what the company hoped to achieve: a three-year agreement with a twenty-five cent per hour increase in the wage progression. Each job classification had a set wage progression beginning at four dollars an hour and progressing with annual increments until top pay was reached in ten years. There were three job titles: installer, technician, and senior technician. With progression through the pay grades, the employee could earn a maximum of ten dollars per hour. It was the practice to negotiate wage increases across the pay grades. If, for example, the average wage was six dollars an hour, a twenty-five cent increase amounted to, roughly, a 4 percent increase. Gordon outlined my authority; I could agree to an increase of twenty-five cents an hour, but we wanted a three-year agreement.

The contact with the IBEW employees was going to expire within a month. A meeting was set up in a motel room in Warren. The union would be represented by an IBEW representative, the local employee representative, their attorney, myself, and a labor attorney that the company engaged. At the meeting, it became immediately clear that the IBEW representative, Mike Namadan, would speak for the employees; our attorney would speak for our company. Mike Namadan was an old-time union organizer; he was about five foot six and built like a bulldog. It was immediately apparent that he was a tough guy who had been through the union wars. He reminded me of a combination of Walter Ruether and Jimmy Hoffa—he was no one's fool. He presented the union proposal: a one-year contract, a 6 percent increase and two additional vacation days. After a short recess, our attorney presented the company's position: a ten-cent an hour increase and a five-year agreement. To this Mike exploded; he threatened a strike and proceeded to say that if there was a strike the entire contract would have to be renegotiated. It was his position that the company was making huge profits on the backs of the working man and he was tired of it. He indicated that he was prepared for a long, violent strike with blood in the street, "if that's what's necessary for the working man to get fair treatment." With that, we adjourned for lunch. Our attorney did not have much to say during lunch; he was hired for this negotiation only.

After lunch, our attorney moved up five cents an hour and cut our contract length demand to three years. After another outburst by Mike, which included an offer to settle this in the street with fists, he lowered his demand to a thirty cents an hour increase, a two-year agreement and two additional vacation days. This negotiation had dragged on all day, and I was getting tired. We took another break. I did not know what to do; I had sat quietly through the meeting while the attorney did the talking. When we resumed, I informed Mike that his offer was unacceptable, if he wanted to settle this he had to lower his demand. After another tirade, I restated our position and another break was called so that both sides could discuss their final offer.

When we resumed, I suggested that the company was willing to increase its money offer if the union would drop the two additional vacation days and agree to a three-year contract. To this Mike responded, "We'll come down to twenty-five

CHAPTER 11

cents an hour and a two-year agreement." To this I responded, "Fine." Immediately Mike called for another recess. I walked out of the meeting room and Mike motioned that I should follow him outside the motel. I did not know what to expect. Mike walked up to me and said, "You don't have much experience at this. This negotiation was going fine until you opened your mouth. What was supposed to happen is that you should have countered with another offer." I told him his offer was within my guidelines; the company wanted a three-year agreement but a two-year agreement was probably okay. Mike continued, "I represent the workers at a local factory employing fifty people. They use this agreement as a model for their wage increase demand. If the factory owners have to pay that much of an increase, it will bankrupt them." "Mike," I said, "What do you want me to do?" "When we return, you say, 'You did not understand my last offer,' and ask me to repeat it. I will restate my offer, and you will say, 'That's not acceptable.'" Then he asked, "What time is your airplane?" The meeting resumed. After another two hours of theatrics, we concluded with a twenty-cent increase per hour and a new contract for three years. I made my airplane flight. The next day when I got to work, Gordon asked me, "How's Mike? You don't have a black eye, so I guess you did alright." I described our new contract; Gordon was pleased. My only comment was, "This was not covered in the AMA course." Gordon chuckled.

During the years I worked for companies, I had several contacts with unions. Fast forward some years while I worked for TelePrompTer Corporation as regional vice president. There was a long, contentious strike by the employees working in Vineland, New Jersey, who were represented by the Teamster Union. The Teamsters were noted for their tough tactics and were headed by Jimmy Hoffa, who at the time of his disappearance was under indictment for corruption and racketeering. He had been investigated for misusing union pension money. The Teamsters were suspected of being controlled by the Mafia. Fortunately, I did not have to handle the negotiation as TelePrompTer had a staff to do this; my job was to direct their efforts. After the strike was settled, I received a call from the local manager; the workers were not working. I asked him to be specific. The employees had a ringleader who developed a code for our two radios. When a supervisor left the office, the dispatcher would press the transmitter once; that meant *get to work*. Once the supervisor returned to the office, a dispatcher would press the transmitter twice. The manager explained that our installation and service work was not getting done; our customers were becoming enraged. I discussed this with Jack Mackey, who handled union negotiations. Jack suggested that I contact the local Teamster representative and request a meeting. I can't remember the representative's name, so I'll call him Tony. I called Tony, and after explaining who I was, I asked to meet with him. He stated, "Bring your attorney and Jack Mackey with you." We drove to the building; it looked like an expensive Italian restaurant. The office we were led to looked like a room in a medieval castle decorated in red and black. Tony was seated at his desk with his attorney next to him. There was no preamble, no greeting, and no inquiry about our trip; "What do you want?" was all that was said. We took it upon ourselves to sit down. I explained what was going on in Vineland. There were no questions, all Tony said was, "Goodbye." When we got outside, I asked Jack what in the world that was all about. Jack explained, "The Mafia keeps close watch on their local representatives. Their dealings are to

CHAPTER 11

be above board." He continued, "If there is criminal activity in the Teamsters, it happens above his level. If Tony was suspected of illicit dealings his days would be numbered." I returned to my office, and several days later the Vineland manager called the dispatcher and the ringleader resigned that morning. The work forces productivity had increased dramatically. This situation was never covered in the AMA labor relations course, but was right out of the Bed-Stuy playbook. I can imagine the conversation with the ringleader and dispatcher. "Maybe you should find another job. Nice kneecaps."

While at TVC, I had the good fortune of working on the first-ever utility rate setting case in the cable television industry. The company applied to the city council of Bellows Falls, Vermont, for a rate increase, as was required by the local franchise. The Public Utilities Commission (PUC) of Vermont asserted jurisdiction. The customers in Bellows Falls thought four dollars per month for cable television service was too much. At that time, I was taking a graduate course at Pace in rate regulation. We engaged a rate consultant, Joe Brennan, to assist. I worked with Joe developing our case many late nights. I had to present the case at a public meeting in Bellows Falls in front of the Vermont PUC. I was determined to have all the facts committed to memory. The local high school auditorium was the venue and it was packed—standing room only. The hearing examiner tried to trip me up at every turn, but I answered each question confidently. Next to talk was our expert witness, Joe Brennan. The line of questioning was fairly straightforward; Joe Brennan knew the procedure well. As it turned out, being a utility, the company could justify a fee of ten dollars per month; the audience was shocked—they were expecting a reduction. As it turned out, we were better prepared than the PUC for the hearing. As Gordon said, the key is preparation.

Working for TVC was a pleasure. The offices were located at La Maison Française, the French building in Rockefeller Center. I had an office overlooking the ice skating rink. With each season, I enjoyed a front row seat as the flora display changed. The company's principal owner was Alfred Stern; his family founded Sears, Roebuck & Company. Mr. Stern was a very mannered, cultured person.

I worked with a number of outstanding professionals. One fellow, Frank Cooper, came up with the concept of selling first-run movies via cable television; this later became HBO. Unfortunately, Frank never received the credit he deserved. It is rare that anyone gets to work on the start of a new business with an untested product. We conducted cable subscriber surveys and extrapolated from these the expected subscription levels, a challenging but fun assignment. TVC acquired a number of cable television systems during my tenure. I worked on the financial analysis; this was an invaluable experience.

In 1972, Warner Communications acquired TVC. I remember the first board of directors meeting. One of the issues discussed was Frank Cooper's project. Also discussed was TVC's European venture. I'd receive telexes (similar to faxes, the closest thing to an email at that time) from Peter Warburton (TVC European representative) with assumptions and I would telex him back the financial analysis. This effort resulted in the company installing cable TV in Asse, Belgium. The initial number of subscribers was near 70 percent and guaranteed the company substantial returns on its investment. It was from Peter, the quintessential English gentleman, that I learned what it meant to "sort it out", i.e., *get things in order*,

CHAPTER 11

and how I could "keep my pecker up", i.e., *don't get discouraged* (an example of two people separated by a common language). The conclusion by the Warner board was that the public was not ready to buy movies at home and that Europe was a waste of time. Many years later, Warner acquired HBO from Time Magazine for several billion dollars—an innovative channel they could have had for free.

An explanation is required at this point: cable television at this time provided television reception service; it was a big antenna system. One industry veteran, Elmer Metz, described cable television as "more and clearer," referring to the television pictures. This was all that a cable television company had to offer. There were no satellite channels (e.g., CNN, ESPN, etc.).

At the same meeting, the construction of the Akron, Ohio, system was discussed and the board thought this was impressive as it would be the largest cable system in the United States when completed. The citizens of Akron received the Cleveland, Ohio, television signals with rabbit ears (small antenna located on top of the TV).

This project was started with great fanfare. Just prior to the sale to Warner, I spent many months in Akron. My job was to establish financial controls, computer billing, accounts payable, and monitor direct sales.

The initial sales success was incredible; in excess of 70 percent of contacts were taking the service. The first two months of service was free for new subscribers. We were selling a giveaway. For this, the salesman received a commission of twenty dollars. I stumbled upon a situation where the salesman actually paid a customer ten dollars to take the service. When customers came to the end of the free trial period, 80 percent disconnected. These results were covered up by ever-increasing sales. The sales report was assembled manually. The computer billing system, unfortunately, was only used after the customer elected to pay for the service. This was a major deficiency in the procedure.

On one trip home from Akron, I ran into Joel Smith (Gordon Fuqua's replacement) at the Cleveland Ohio Airport. Joel and I discussed the Akron project on the plane ride home. When I told him my findings, he concluded that construction must be stopped until we found a way to attract and hold customers. The next day, Joel told me he was going to see Mr. Stern and put a halt to the project. Upon Joel's return to the office from his meeting with Mr. Stern, I asked him what happened. He didn't answer and walked into his office; the Akron project continued. It was obvious that Mr. Stern did not want this information known because of the pending sale. About one month later, Warner purchased TVC. The Akron project was one of the major reasons for the acquisition. Warner could claim that it was the proud owner of the nation's largest cable television company (i.e., they had the best seat on the Titanic).

I had a conversation with Jim Cantor, a Warner vice president; he had worked his way up in Warner by marrying the sister of Steve Ross, who was president of Warner. During our talk, he told me that the "tubes had to be cleared of all nonproductive people." It was clear that he was referring to me. I thought, *What a helpful comment.* I typically worked between fifty and sixty hours a week and travelled frequently. (Note: Several years later, Jim Cantor divorced Steve Ross's sister and was fired from Warner.)

What stood out most about the Warner Board meetings was that all the Board members wore Gucci loafers. My conservative wing tips did not mesh well with this. During a whirlwind

CHAPTER 11

airplane tour of the country on the Warner jet, I resigned. I thought we were going to crash in Menominee, Michigan. The weather was bad but the Warner people, including Steve Ross, thought we had to land despite the fact the pilot had missed the runway on his first pass. A lot of office worker machismo. I'll never forget how he brought that plane around as if it were a fighter jet.

That was a bunch of dogs I did not lie down with. (Note: Several months later the plane did crash, but it was hushed up as the plane was used to ferry stars such as Barbara Streisand around the country. Fortunately, no one was killed.)

I didn't have another job when I resigned. During the time I was looking for employment, I did tax returns and consulting. One of my projects was for a client who had purchased a cable television system. He was looking for a way to write off the purchase price and get a tax deduction. At that time, the largest portion of the purchase price was considered goodwill, i.e., non-tax deductible. I came up with a formula for the useful life of a cable television subscriber, much the way a newspaper subscriber is valued when the paper is sold. The client used this and was successful in convincing the IRS that this was tax deductible. I understand that this method is still used to value acquired cable television customers. I guess I've left my mark. I also did tax returns in a small office in the south Bronx, a job I would not recommend.

Chapter 12

Adelphia Communications
June 1973

I interviewed for a position as vice president and comptroller with John Rigas, President of Adelphia Communications, in a hotel suite in New York City. This position required that I relocate to Coudersport, Pennsylvania, where Adelphia was headquartered. I visited Coudersport, was offered the position, and I accepted. This was quite a change moving to a small rural town with a population of around two thousand people. By this time, we had James, Bernard and Marie. My family handled the relocation fairly well.

We arrived in Coudersport in June of 1973. Things went well for the first six months. Adelphia was a new company, with all the problems that accompany a new venture. We had purchased a nice home that was walking distance from the office. The office at that time consisted of two office girls, John Rigas, and me, and it was located over the Western Auto Store in downtown Coudersport.

At that time, Arthur Burns was chairman of the Federal Reserve and, to correct the economy, interest rates were increased to unprecedented levels. This was a major problem for Adelphia as the interest rate on its debt was tied to the prime rate: every time the rate increased, Adelphia had to pay more. Near the end of my first year with Adelphia, John engaged a consultant to assist the company in securing a new lender at lower interest rates. It required many hours preparing financial projections. The company had made a lot of progress since I started. We had an accounting system, a customer billing system, and the company was beginning to pay its bills, although money was extremely tight.

One day John walked into the office and was going through the outgoing mail. In a loud voice he asked, "Who is sending out these checks? We can't afford this!" then ripped the checks up and stormed out of the office. I don't know who John thought wrote the checks, as I was the only person in the office who could write a check. The checks he tore up were for the withheld payroll taxes. When John came back to the office, I explained to him that the withheld taxes must be paid. This was not the company's money, it was money withheld from the employees' paychecks and belonged to the government. He said we needed to conserve our cash and he would "deal with the consequences."

Within a few days, he told me to write a check to a consultant for five thousand dollars and that the company was going to have to pay this each month until the new financing was arranged. I began to feel uncomfortable. My suspicions were confirmed when I overheard John's brother ask him if he had got their check from the consultant. There were several other stockholders in Adelphia. Between John and his brother, they owned slightly more than 50 percent of the stock. They were defrauding the stockholders and violating the loan agreement. I began to reach out to people I knew in the cable industry for a new job.

CHAPTER 12

The matter came to a head the day an IRS auditor walked into the office and announced that he was there to collect the payroll taxes. There was a back door to the office. I heard it open and close; John bugged out. The agent asked who I was and I told him. He stated that he would leave with a check for the withheld taxes or the keys to my house. I immediately made out the check. A few hours later John came back to the office and asked what had happened. I informed him that the withheld taxes were paid to the IRS. A few days later, I told John I was leaving the company and that he was personally going to buy the stock I had been promised when I was hired. He did.

I should have known that Adelphia and I had no future. We had moved to Coudersport in June and at the end of August my son James asked, "This has been a great vacation. When are we going home?" As they say, wisdom comes "out of the mouths of babes."

Professionally, the year I worked for Adelphia was the worst five years of my career.

To explain my last comment above, I'll tell you a Texas story. A cowboy is told by his doctor that he has only six months to live. To this the cowboy says, "Is there anything I can do?" After some thought the doctor responds, "Well, you can marry an ugly woman and move to Oklahoma." The cowboy asks, "Will doing this make me live longer?" Again after some thought the doctor responds, "Well, no, but it will feel longer."

Chapter 13

Return to New York

The years since the navy were productive for me. I had completed my college education and had established a career while our family of five prospered. I could not have accomplished this without the help of Diane. Returning to New York ushered in a new beginning and, in retrospect, the beginning of the end of our marriage. We moved to New City in Rockland County because Diane's cousin lived there. We had visited and liked the area, the school system was rated very well, and all these things were important to us. We found a house that was within our price range and were excited about living in the New York area again. I would have to commute to Manhattan each day but didn't think it would be a problem.

New Yorkers measure how far they are from Manhattan in time; the trip from New City took one and a half hours, a distance of thirty miles. I'd leave the house at 6:30 am and arrive home between 7:00 and 8:00 pm, unless I worked overtime. I had no time for my family during the week. On weekends, I was usually brain dead from long days at the office and the mind-numbing commute home. This began to wear on our marriage.

A couple of years after moving to New City, Diane returned to school and got a master's degree. She applied for and received a position with General Foods as a research biologist (her field of study). To her credit, she did this while balancing home and family, as I was generally MIA (missing in action). Our lives were beginning to take separate paths.

Beginning in 1974, I was the cub master of our local Cub Scout Pack. My son, James, had joined the Cub Scouts while we lived in Coudersport. When we moved to New City, I went with him to sign him up with the local pack. At the meeting, the organizer said that they did not have a cub master as the current fellow had just had a heart attack. With that I said to James, "Let's go home." He looked at me with a tear in his eye and said "Daddy, you mean I can't be in the Cub Scouts?" The hours I worked were excruciating and the commute meant that I rarely got home before 7:00 pm. I had no idea how I'd fulfill the commitment, but I raised my hand and said I would take the job as cub master. When he was old enough, my son Bernard also joined the pack. Our times spent together I'll always treasure.

The Cub Scout Pack was nearly out of business when we started. Within five years, the pack had thirty-five boys and adult volunteers for all positions. Countless times, I just barely made the monthly meeting at 7:00 pm on Friday night after getting off a plane from a business trip and running through the house to get into my uniform. These were some of the best years we had as a family. Twice, I and four other fathers took the pack to visit Washington D.C., and each year we had a father-son camping trip.

Whenever possible, I'd take my children hiking or canoeing. My daughter Marie was my most consistent partner. We

CHAPTER 13

hiked many miles of the Appalachian Trail. The trail crosses Bear Mountain State Park, roughly thirty miles from our home at the time. On one hike, we climbed an area known as "the staircase." On the map, it's described as almost perpendicular. To a small girl this must have appeared to be Mount Everest. With me behind her, she climbed straight up—only later did I realize how frightening this must have been. Several times, we rented canoes and paddled down the Delaware River. On one trip, the canoe got stuck between two large rocks, and we had to be rescued by a river guide. Another trip with Marie years later, skiing in Angel Fire, New Mexico, was memorable. It was so cold that Marie's tears froze her eyelashes together and I had to hold my hand over her eyes to melt the ice. These trips were priceless.

I missed many birthdays and special events because of my work schedule. I can't recall what was so important at work, but it pains me to think how I must have disappointed my children.

My years with the Cub Scouts are one thing I'm proud of. When my son James married Tracey, they had a large wedding party. Several of the ushers came up to me and asked if I remembered our trips to Washington and our camping trips, and said how much they had enjoyed the activities.

One's rewards are not always measured in dollars.

Chapter 14

Teleprompter

Through a business contact I had at TelePrompTer (a three-part company: cable TV systems, music service, and telephone interconnect), I secured a position as director of capital budgets. My family, as they had in the past, soldiered on as we settled into New City and I continued to work long hours. The fellow that helped me secure this position was Jerry Greene. I met Jerry when I was working on the acquisition of Cypress Communications by Warner. As it turned out, I was the first person through the door after Warner purchased Cypress. Cypress was located in Los Angles. My assignment was to begin transitioning Cypress to our budget system. After several weeks, broken up with mid-week flights back to New York for meetings, I was able to produce a budget that conformed to the Warner system. One observation I made to Jerry was that after reviewing the Cypress procedures, it appeared that Cypress should be buying our company. Cypress had excellent automated accounting and billing procedures, while the Warner systems for the most part were manual. Several years later, Jerry Greene was killed in a small airplane crash while rushing back to New York in a storm for a meeting that "could not wait." Had he lived, I'm certain he would have made a significant mark in the industry.

My years at TelePrompTer were stressful and in a typical week I worked in excess of sixty hours. My initial job was capital budgeting. The assignment was to cut spending. TelePrompTer was on the verge of bankruptcy when I started with them in 1974. Each day I received a stack of purchase orders and had to decide if the order was necessary. The guideline was "spend only what is needed to keep the systems operating." At that time, TelePrompTer was the largest cable operator in the U.S. and had over one million subscribers spread across the country. The hours were long and the commute from New City was tormenting, but I was committed to doing a good job.

In my second year at TelePrompTer, I was promoted to northeast regional manager. This came about when John Raines resigned from his position. When I heard about this, I went to Bill Bresnan, president of the cable division, and told him I wanted the job and knew I could handle it. He agreed with me.

Being promoted to regional manager was a shock to most of my fellow employees. I've learned that if you see an opportunity, act on it and don't worry what others will think. I will always be grateful to Bill Bresnan for giving me that opportunity.

Prior to TelePrompTer, my jobs were accounting or finance related. I have a degree in accounting, but I struggled to get marginal grades in accounting in college. I can't do simple math; I sometimes transpose numbers (as I stated before, a mild case of dyslexia). This would probably discourage most people from pursuing a career crunching numbers, but widespread understanding about dyslexia had not yet caught on back then, and so I never labeled it as a drawback. Later, I

CHAPTER 14

realized I didn't want to do accounting, not because of my dyslexia, but because I found it boring.

When Bernard was a baby, he had an ear infection and blockage that took over a year to diagnose and another year to cure. As a result, he had a gap in his development that showed up in grammar school, and he had a difficult time. He struggled with this for many years but was never defeated by this affliction. He graduated from Pace University (formerly Pace College when I attended) in less than four years completing bachelor's and master's degrees while taking the honors program and working twenty hours a week. Today he is a CPA and chief accounting officer of a large investment company. As it turns out, my grandson Brendan (Bernard's son), had a similar hearing problem and is a straight-A student having worked through speech and hearing therapy. He is a bright and cheerful young man. It's no coincidence that three generations have had to overcome similar problems. My point in mentioning this is that, "you are dealt a hand of cards and you're measured by how well you play your hand." It troubles me when I hear someone blame an affliction for a lifetime of failure. Many would read the line "to profit by affliction" from *What I Live For* and scratch their head; my family understands its meaning.

At TelePrompTer, I began to understand how to manage a cable television business. After a year as regional manager, I was promoted to vice president. I had operational responsibility for over forty cable television systems serving 400,000 customers in twenty states. As regional vice president, I was responsible for all aspects of the business: finance, marketing, personnel, and engineering. I reported to the cable division president, but this was a loose structure. I ran the region as if it were my own business.

I had been in my new position for about a year when the marketing manager for my region resigned. We advertised in the Wall Street Journal and received about twenty-five résumés. I was reading through the applicants and one stood out—his name was John Lynch. Coincidentally, that was the name of the assistant engineering officer on the USS *Remey*. Looking at Lynch's background disclosed that it was in fact the same John Lynch that used to come down to the engine room and say, "Okay, you animals, put your backs into it!" I don't think he would have said that in front of the engineering officer, who was a decent man and treated us with respect.

I was tempted to have him come in for an interview and let one of the "animals" turn him down for a job. I labored over this for several days and finally I threw the résumé in the garbage. He wasn't qualified for the job and I wasn't going to rub his nose in it.

I've had a few other similar encounters like this in my life. Another person who called me up looking for a job was Mike Joyce (my supervisor at Vikoa). We did not have any position for him but I tried to advise him. I don't believe that you should exact retribution for every wrong, and I believe that to do so, when another person is in need, diminishes you. Be thankful for what you have.

TelePrompTer was divided into three regions. There were ongoing construction needs. We had a small crew in the northeast region headed by Al Rogers, a good construction man. The western region had large construction projects and, Western Region Vice President, WR, V.P., asked if he could recruit Al Rogers because he did not have a construction

CHAPTER 14

foreman on staff. After discussing this, it was decided that Al would transfer. The WR, V.P. had come up through the company starting as technician, and had been promoted several times. When I met the WR V.P., he let me know that he was a "born-again Christian." Personally, he and I did not get along; he did not care for Catholics and he let me know it.

About a year after Al's transfer, I heard that he had been injured on the job and was in the hospital. I telephoned Al to offer my condolences. During the conversation, he informed me that he had been terminated. I confronted the WR V.P.; "How could you terminate a man injured on the job?" His response was, "I have my budget to worry about." I was so mad, the only thing I could think to say was, "I hope someday you work for a Christian just like yourself." I had Al reinstated and transferred back to the northeast region. The way the disability law worked was that once a person was disabled, they received a disability check (approximately 80 percent of their regular salary), but that meant that the employee was no longer employed and would lose all of the other company benefits. It was not difficult to convince Al that when he received his disability check, he could turn it over to the company, and would receive his regular salary and maintain his company benefits. After recuperation, Al returned to work in the region. I heard that after the WR, V.P. left TelePrompTer, he was working for a new start-up company and was discharged without notice. I guess his new boss had his budget to worry about. I believe the world pays you back for your deeds. You reap what you sow.

In early 1978, a problem developed in the cable system in Presque Isle, Maine. A local group had formed for the purpose of obtaining a competing franchise and constructing a new cable system to compete with the TelePrompTer system.

Despite what might have been a popular belief at that time, operating cable systems was not that profitable. There was a constant need to introduce new technologies and services. The market constraints of revenue were sufficient to keep rates low.

There had been some sensational cases in the press of rate-increase abuses by cable operators, but these were few. One case was seized upon by Al Gore (then a United States senator), which gave him a political platform. His grandmother lived in a small Tennessee town where the cable system owner increased the rates by a substantial amount without proper justification. His argument had some merit but not enough to damn an entire industry. TelePrompTer was "painted with the same tar brush" by the city manager of Presque Isle.

There was no way competing cable systems could survive and make money. A second cable system in Presque Isle would cause TelePrompTer substantial financial and public relations damage. Cities that granted competing franchises did so because the existing cable provider was doing a poor job and its citizens were demanding action. If a competing franchise was granted, my days at TelePrompTer were numbered. This suspicion was reinforced when at one of our management luncheons Bill Bresnan asked, "How is your problem in Presque Isle, Jim?" I organized a top to bottom review of the Presque Isle operation and spent several weeks working with the manager and talking to our customers. We did a door-to-door survey of customer opinions, attitudes and service complaints. I had a feeling that the operation was being well run; now I had to have proof. The customers were very positive about the local operation and were well satisfied with the service. We had our facts and were well prepared. I met with the city manager, Dana Connors. In conversations with a local attorney,

CHAPTER 14

he disclosed that Dana was promoting the group who applied for the competing franchise. There was a city council meeting scheduled to decide the fate of the competing franchise. Armed with all my data, the local manager, Earl Davis, and I went to the meeting.

We had worked out an agenda for the meeting: Earl would present the survey results and I would discuss the economic impact on the community that this second franchise would have. We had a good case.

At the council meeting, it was obvious that Dana had scripted it in advance. When it was TelePrompTer's time to speak, Dana completely ignored the agreed-upon agenda and in his best Yankee accent said, "This here New Yorker has come up here to hoodwink you," and proceeded to introduce me. I began my presentation and said, "Well, I don't know if I can 'hood-wink' you," going on to explain that I was very familiar with Presque Isle and that I had, in fact, visited the area in my youth, and that during one such visit I had dug out my uncle's outhouse. One of the council members stopped me with, "Who is your uncle?" I responded, "George Keyes." The councilman said, "How is old George? I bought a refrigerator off him twenty-five years ago and it still works." Furthermore, he added, "You know George had a rough time of it and left town owing some folks money. Over the years he's paid them all back." After a few minutes of conversation about how this competing franchise could hurt the existing operation that was providing excellent service, the councilmen made a motion to table the competing franchise. It passed unanimously.

There were several franchise problems that TelePrompTer had to overcome. Prior to 1973, the then president of TelePrompTer, Irving Kahn, was convicted of bribing local officials in Johnstown, Pennsylvania, to obtain a renewal of TelePrompTer's franchise to operate. At that time, the loss of a franchise would have damaged their business and could have led to bankruptcy. I had met Mr. Kahn several times; he was thought to be a "brilliant" cable operator. (I'm always annoyed when people equate business success as brilliance. I don't think it's brilliance; it's craftiness. Mozart was brilliant. When it comes to business people, painfully few are brilliant. Most just pay attention.)

You did not talk to Irving, you listened. I'll admit, he had detailed knowledge of the technology and a clear vision of where the industry was headed. Before anyone had thought about it, Irving had concluded that satellite communications would revolutionize cable television and that a system carrying telephone, as well as video, was in the future. I think back to what my uncle would say: "Educated you might be; smart you're not." Irving had business skills, and had a vision of the industry, but he couldn't deal with people. He had no confidence in those that worked for him, so the ones that reported to him at the corporate level were drones. He was insightful about things, but failed to see his greatest asset: his people.

The Johnstown franchise was in limbo and was in my region. Because of the corruption and federal charges, the Federal Communications Commission (FCC) inserted itself into the franchise renewal process. The investigation came to a head in the mid-1970s. A hearing was called by the FCC in Johnstown. TelePrompTer was required to carry the hearing on its local origination channel. The hearing examiner opened the meeting, stating that it was the FCC's intention to hear all the evidence against TelePrompTer and take the necessary steps to void the franchise. With that, the public was invited

CHAPTER 14

to appear on camera and speak their piece. The first person to appear was a local priest who praised the local manager, Walt Kinash, for making the company channel available to them. This was followed by local citizens who praised the service, the union who talked about how fair the company treated their employees, and a Johnstown councilman who expressed his gratitude to Walt for the way he always responded to local concerns. As it turned out, there was no way that the TelePrompTer franchise was not going to be renewed. After two hours of testimony, the FCC hearing examiner ended the meeting. The franchise was renewed within two weeks.

This is a good example of why you should respect the efforts of others. Mr. Kahn had not even discussed the franchise with the local manager—he knew what was best; after all, he was "brilliant." I met with Irving Kahn after he got out of jail. He had invested in a cable television business in New Jersey. It was part of my region and we were working on developing a statewide channel that would be carried exclusively by New Jersey cable televisions. He was a cable TV operator in the state and had gotten himself on the committee that was developing the channel. Several cable TV executives and I met with Irving. He spent the entire meeting railing against the current management of TelePrompTer and bragging how he had become rich because he sold his stock prior to the indictment. With respect to the new channel he knew what was best. After he had stopped talking, he ended the meeting. I do know that the system he was developing in New Jersey had to be sold to the New York Times and that Irving lost money on the sale. A channel was developed for the state of New Jersey; Irving was not part of the founding consortium group. He still did not get it. What good is all the money in the world if you soil your name? One of the reasons we were successful in Presque Isle was that our local manager had done such an excellent job. To this day, I'm glad I'm not "brilliant" and listened to what our customers and local employees had to say. Too many times business people believe their own press releases.

During the first year I worked at TelePrompTer, I was talking to my cousin Peter Berkowitz. It was clear he needed to begin establishing himself in a career. I set up an interview for him and he began as a management trainee in Oswego, New York. As it turned out, by the time I became regional manager, Peter was managing one of the company's larger systems—Wildwood, New Jersey. As a manager, Peter was excellent. Part of my compensation was my annual bonus. In bad years, I could always count on Pete to deliver the earnings. Not only do I owe Peter for my first bicycle, I owe him for my bonuses. He is one of my best friends.

TelePrompTer was a nationwide network of cable systems. The industry at that time was mostly restricted to rural areas, prior to satellite-delivered television programming. TelePrompTer was in a partnership with Hughes Aircraft and had built a cable system in northern Manhattan. Because of the need to carry more than thirteen channels, a converter box was developed (i.e., a device that would allow for the distribution of more than the standard thirteen channels). The days of the television dial were about to end and remote controls were to become the norm. Because of the structure of this deal, it was not included in my region, and reported to its own board of directors.

After the resignation of the regional vice president for the southwest region, a fellow that had worked for Sony Corporation, Dave MacDonald, was brought in to replace

CHAPTER 14

him. Dave had been in sales at a high level with Sony. At a management luncheon at TelePrompTer's corporate office, we discussed the converter usage in the Manhattan cable TV system. It was agreed that, while we were able to build converters, it was not something an operating company like TelePrompTer should be involved with. The conversation led Dave to contact Sony to discuss manufacturing converters.

A meeting was set up with Mr. Morita, president and founder of Sony. He arrived at the meeting with an assistant. It was my task to drive him to the Manhattan cable office and give him a tour. He said very little. When we got back to our office, he told us he would have some of his people contact us. About one month later, a group of ten people arrived from Sony. They went through every inch of the operation. One of the engineers asked if he could have a converter box to take with him. Naturally, we said yes. Each month we'd ask Dave at the management luncheon if he'd heard anything from Sony. After a while, it fell off the agenda; we guessed that they were not interested. About one year after the entourage's visit, Sony introduced the cable-ready television set, capable of carrying more than thirteen channels. Another example of Sony's pioneering research. Every time I think of this, I'm reminded of the scene in a WWII movie where the Japanese pilot lines up behind the U.S. fighter plane and says as he fires his guns: "Here, take back the Third Avenue El, Yank." Just prior to WWII, the Japanese had purchased the scrap steel from the old 3rd Avenue El, which was being taken down. They must have used some of the metal in their ammunitions. The Japanese are very good at using American technology and materials to their advantage.

While at TelePrompTer, the cable TV industry moved from a rural-only business to the larger cities. Only one person deserves credit for this—Ted Turner. He introduced the first satellite-delivered television channels: WTBS-Atlanta and CNN. Though there is much to applaud Turner for, there was also another side.

It was important to Turner that his new satellite-delivered services be carried on TelePrompTer's cable systems. He courted the people at TelePrompTer with offers to come to Newport, Rhode Island, and go sailing with him, and in one case arranged box seats at the World Series. I never accepted his offers. Our vice president of marketing was enthralled with the opportunity to be with someone famous. I remember him telling me of his weekend excursion with Ted and all the "beautiful people" (my description of the people at the sailing event).

After the first introduction of Turner's CNN, an imitator decided to broadcast a competing service. That was Group W. Concurrent with this, Group W began talks of purchasing TelePrompTer. Turner Broadcasting launched a lawsuit to block the transaction and cited information that could only have come from insiders. All of the vice presidents were grilled. At the end of this process, the vice president of marketing was terminated.

Maybe it was Turner, not Al Pacino in the movie *The Godfather*, who originally came up with, "Keep your friends close, but keep your enemies closer." Of one thing I'm certain; after reading that Turner had married Jane Fonda, I observed life has a way of exacting justice for what you do. Myself, I prefer mercy.

Group W (i.e., Westinghouse) made an offer to purchase TelePrompTer at around thirty-six dollars per share. This offer

CHAPTER 14

was accepted and the announcement was made. The staff was gathered in the large conference room. We heard from Russell Karp (president of TelePrompTer) and Bill Bresnan (president of TelePrompTer Cable) that they were excited and had been meeting with "Dan." This turned out to be Dan Richey, president of Group W; Bill and Russ were already on a first-name basis with the new boss. This seemed strange, as the deal had been made without their knowledge by Jack Kent Cooke, majority stockholder of TelePrompTer. Immediately my antenna went up and I thought, *This does not sound right.*

There was a series of meetings scheduled with groups of us to discuss what the new company expected. To go into all of that is a waste of space, as you will see.

A trip was scheduled to visit a nearby cable operation (i.e., Newburgh, New York) with Dan Richey. As this was my area, I had to accompany an entourage to Newburgh. One person Dan stopped to talk with was the office manager. She ran a busy office in a difficult town. I had spent many days in Newburgh because the cable system was falling apart. Nothing ensures customer ire better than poor service. This always shows up in the stress level of the office. I knew she did the best she could. On the way out of the office Dan said, "Get rid of her," as if this poor lady was responsible for our lousy technical service, which, of course, she was not.

Throughout the years we had presented plans to upgrade the technical quality of the cable systems. When cash was tight and we had to get by, we did so. For the last couple of years before the Group W sale, the company had been generating sufficient cash to begin the process of rebuilding. I would present a budget plan that included needed equipment upgrades to "Russ" and "Bill." This was an annual charade. We would prepare the plan and have never-ending meetings with Karp, Bresnan and a bevy of financial staff. After this was complete, the plan would be forwarded to Jack Kent Cooke. The operating goals were always increased and the upgrades rejected.

I remember one project that illustrates how the procedure worked. The cable television system (i.e., electronics, cable wire, and fittings) that serviced the Elmira, New York, subscribers was about 20 years old. In some areas, the strand cable was so corroded that the cable technicians had to use baling wire to support the cable. Around 1975, we requested a rate increase and had to appear before the city council. During the hearing, the council pointed out the obvious problems with the system. I told them I was aware of the problems and that we would work to maintain the existing system, and that after another rate increase next year the system would be rebuilt. The council agreed. The rebuild would pay for itself. When "Jack" looked at the budget, he turned it down. His comment was, "The team that is losing works harder than the winning team." If this seems confusing to the reader, it certainly was to me. What that comment had to do with rebuilding a cable system I'll never know. To this day, I dislike the sports metaphors used to describe business tactics.

The senior management of TelePrompTer was terrified of Mr. Cooke. During one of his visits to the New York office he observed that one of the employees had his door closed. I guess he felt that someone with the door closed had something to hide or was plotting against him. The fellow with the closed door designed advertising and needed quiet to concentrate. Mr. Cooke had his assistant terminate him on the spot. Mr. Cooke was a short man and I think he had a Napoleon complex. During one of our meetings, a secretary came in,

CHAPTER 14

and said that Mr. Cooke was on the telephone and wanted to talk to a person at the meeting. We normally worked in our shirtsleeves but always kept a suit jacket with us as Mr. Cooke thought that his executives should always wear a suit jacket. That person got up and put on his jacket before picking up the telephone. I thought, *That's fear*. Just the thought of talking to him and not being appropriately dressed was unthinkable.

The one redeeming feature of the TelePrompTer method of operation was that after the annual budget comedy, I was free to do what I wanted so long as I met the budgeted objectives. I made things work and the region always met or exceeded budgeted income.

When the integration of Group W began, one comment I heard was that our operations were terrible. The commenter, upon realizing what he said, immediately stated, "You guys are great." My reasoning went: *The operations are terrible, I'm great, and I'm responsible for operations, which are terrible.* I remember my college logic course; this reasoning did not make sense. He also stated that the TelePrompTer executives were going to be offered an employment contract. I never had an employment contract before and could not understand why I needed one now. Contracts are commonplace in our modern age, but back then, you just did your job, whatever that entailed. It was "employment at will" (i.e., willfully employed)—a mutually satisfactory arrangement that doesn't need contracts. As I've said before, *you take the man's dollar, do the man's job*. The world I grew up in was one where a man's word and handshake bound an agreement. It was sufficient.

Chapter 15

Cablevision Industries

As the fates would have it, I had a conversation with Frank Cooper about the state of affairs at TelePrompTer. Things were not going well. This led to an interview with Alan Gerry. I drove up to Liberty, New York, to meet with Alan and we hit it off. I was a little tentative. We had several meetings in June of 1981 and we came to an agreement: I would be employed by Cablevision Industries with the goal of becoming its president.

Before I left TelePrompTer, I sarcastically said to one of the Group W executives that I knew the operations were "terrible." When I started with TelePrompTer the stock was selling at $3.50 per share and Group W was paying $36.00 per share; we must have done something right. After I had given my notice, several people told me I was crazy; that Group W was a big company with lots of money to spend on upgrading the cable systems and were offering an employment contract. The future, to everyone but me, looked bright.

Through the years, I've developed faith in my gut instincts. As I said, I was suspicious of the contract. *Why do you need them? You're the buying company.* These feelings, plus the opportunity to be president of a company, made my decision to leave TelePrompTer easy. My suspicions of Group W proved correct. After I had been at Cablevision Industries for about six months, I heard what happened. The reason Group W offered the contracts was that their banks required assurance that the management of TelePrompTer would be there to run the business, as Group W did not have any employees with cable television experience. Shortly after the acquisition was complete, they rented a floor in the building where TelePrompTer had its office and one by one the TelePrompTer "contract" people were moved to this floor, with instructions to use the desk provided and draw their salary until the contract period was over. One man I knew well was Dick Sykes; he was the treasurer who replaced Jerry Greene. I know that at that time Dick had never looked for a job. He was recruited out of college by a large accounting firm, worked there ten years, and was recruited by TelePrompTer where he put in another ten years. During our conversation, it became obvious that Dick was at his wit's end. Concurrent with this, his wife was divorcing him. I asked Dick to come up to Liberty, New York. When he arrived, we visited with Alan Gerry, who gave Dick some advice about finding another position and I explained to him how to prepare his résumé and begin looking for another job. It was awful to see such a fine man humiliated.

I know that when Group W sold its cable operation, they lost a substantial amount of money. The attitude of the Group W executives was incredible; they thought they knew better than the people at TelePrompTer how to operate the business and had condescended to keep the TelePrompTer employees in order to get their financing. I had heard Dan Richey describe how he terminated people: "Sometimes you have to say, 'Gee fella, you've got to go.'" This cavalier attitude, when deal-

CHAPTER 15

ing with someone's life, sickened me. One lesson I've learned is that everyone's business looks easy until you have to run it yourself. When Group W sold TelePrompTer they lost nearly one billion dollars on the sale. I wonder if this failure made a lasting impression on the Group W people. I doubt it; they played business with other people's money.

I started at Cablevision Industries in June 1981. The headquarters were in Liberty, approximately seventy-five miles from my home in New City, New York. The drive was one and a half hours each way. After the years I had commuted to Manhattan, this ride was a pleasure. I'd listen to the radio, drink coffee, and plan my day. For the most part, there was no traffic and the roads were good.

Cablevision Industries (CI) was founded by Alan Gerry who had started his career installing television antennas on apartment buildings in the Bronx. He was the quintessential self-made man. The CI offices were in an old mill house that Alan had restored; it was decorated by him and full of genuine Tiffany fixtures. When you walked into the CI offices you knew you were in a special place.

There were two definite sides to Alan Gerry. He was the sophisticated head of a very successful company. When he dealt with the Wall Street investment bankers, he was one of them, and they treated him with respect. During our first interview in his gorgeous office, I noticed he had a Marine Corps plaque. When he saw me looking at it he said, "I joined the Marines during World War II to kill Japs, but they ended the war before I had a chance." One time, he asked me to come with him to a rate increase hearing in the town of Wallkill. A person in Alan's position rarely attended these meetings; there was a large staff to handle this type of meeting. On our ride to the meeting, Alan explained that he had started his business in this area and everyone knew him; sending someone else would be considered an insult. The ride to Wallkill was on a snow- and ice-covered road and took about half an hour. During the drive, Alan was extremely animated and drove with abandon. After a white-knuckle ride, we arrived unharmed. When Alan rose to talk, everyone listened. In that area, it was common knowledge that Alan was very wealthy. During his presentation, one of the commissioners practically accused Alan of lying; the veneer came off, the old Marine came out, and Alan said, "Let's settle this in the street." The meeting was immediately taken over by the supervisor, who thanked Alan for taking his valuable time to visit with them on this important matter—the rate increase was approved.

He was one of the most generous employers anyone would want to work for. If one of his employees had an illness, he personally saw to it that they received the best care possible. A design engineer was in the hospital slowly dying of cancer. He made sure that he had his design table set up in his room so that when he was able he could keep himself busy. He kept the designer on his payroll to the very end. At other times, he was unbearable. Once he brought a cable TV broker, Jim DiSorento, to a meeting with his senior staff (the management people of his company). We were discussing the franchising for the Boston area, a complex process. At one point he said, "If I only had some people with brains I would not have to solve all the problems." I thought that a comment like this in front of an outsider was inappropriate and insulting.

Working for Alan reinforced a belief of mine regarding time: *Use it well, for it is the one thing we can't buy more of.*

CHAPTER 15

Each year Alan would write on an easel in his office three or four projects he was going to work on. The list could include financing an expansion, upgrading or rebuilding one of the cable systems, developing a marketing campaign, dealing with a competing cable system, etc. The company employed hundreds of personnel to sell, service, and bill the customers. The only time Alan would get involved with these functions was when there was a problem that only he could solve. He did not waste his time on issues that his staff could handle.

After I had established my own company in Lockney, we were busy adding customers and building or acquiring new cable systems. One day Danny Smith came into my office all excited. Apparently, someone who Danny had worked with had constructed a cable system competing (this was referred to in the cable industry as an "overbuild") with one of Alan's cable systems and was taking Alan's customers with ease. Danny thought that we should join in this effort, as it appeared to be an easy way to grow our business. I told Danny that we would not participate in this and to tell his friend never contact us about it again, and to let his friend find out what it's like to compete with Alan Gerry. Danny mentioned that Alan had recently been overbuilt in Florida by Florida Power and Light (FPL) and they also met little resistance from the local CI employees.

I paid little attention to this until about a year later when Danny informed me that his friend who had overbuilt Alan had been forced out of the business and was now bankrupt. In addition, Alan had purchased FPL's competing cable system at less than cost, and had his construction staff turn off the competing system and remove their cable system from the telephone poles. I told Danny about Alan's annual list of projects.

FPL and his friend had found out what happens when you get on Alan's list. Today, you hear much about multi-tasking; this is one modern practice that I hope goes away. Concentrated effort on important tasks will lead to success, while fragmented effort is just that and wastes time.

There were problems from the start working for Alan. I came from the corporate world; CI presented a cosmopolitan look, but was really a "good old boy" outfit. When I first started at CI, we were working on a project (its contents are not important) and we had a deadline. We needed some critical information from the engineering department. I went looking for the engineers and could not find them. I was told that this was the first day of deer season. My response was, "You've got to be kidding."

During one discussion with Alan, he became agitated and threw a clip on his desk that hit me. I was so outraged I don't remember what was said. Another time, I was by the entrance and Alan bounced through the front door, tossed his car keys at me, and said, "Get my bags out of the car." I never got the bags.

There was a definite deterioration in our relationship during my employment. I believe Alan was sincere when he said that he wanted to slow down and have a professional president run his company. On paper I was that person; in reality I was not.

I did participate in the growth of CI from approximately 250,000 customers when I started, to nearly 500,000 when I left. After I left and achieved a measure of success, I heard that "Alan taught (me) everything (I knew)." Well, that's not quite true. I did learn one thing. On each desk in the CI office was a small plaque that said, "Do it now." This has stayed with me. Whenever I find myself procrastinating, I think of Alan's plaque.

CHAPTER 15

One of the greatest things that had happened to me while I worked at CI was meeting Denise Bertholf. We worked together for over two years and developed a friendship, which later progressed to a romantic relationship. During the period of time between when this started and I told Diane that I was going to leave her was the most tormented time I can remember. I informed Diane that I was leaving her in early January 1983. When I told her, her response was, "I thought you'd wait until all of the children were out of high school." It was not a surprise.

I deeply regretted how I handled this. When asked if I would do anything different with my life, I always say no, but add, *There are some things I wish I had done better.* Handling the divorce is at the top of the list.

When it became apparent that I was not going to be the president, Alan proposed that we form a partnership and sell and install satellite dishes. We formed a company called Sky Channels. In retrospect this was a very generous thing for Alan to do.

Sky Channels was a "hands-on" job. It was a small start-up business, which Alan funded. Prior to this, I had never spliced or installed cable. I had been a typical big company executive that could talk about a "good day's work" but had no idea what that entailed. We had a five-person team: I was the head of the company, Denise and George Slaver handled sales, and Keith Bertholf (my would-be future brother-in-law) and another man were technicians. The way it ran was everyone worked on everything, including me. I gained hands-on experience. During the year that we worked Sky Channels, we sold and installed about $500,000 in earth stations. The winter of 1982-83 was probably the coldest winter we'd seen in many years. One day it was so cold that when I picked up a pipe, it stuck to my bare hands.

In the spring of 1983, Alan and I had a meeting to discuss the future of Sky Channels. I'd worked hard to make a go of it, but realized that this is not what I wanted to do and that the profit potential of this business was limited and said so to Alan. We then met with Alan's attorney, Laz Levine, and came to a settlement for my equity in CI, a four-year payout. After we settled, Alan asked me what I intended to do. I had been thinking of going into business for myself, building or acquiring cable television systems. Alan mentioned that he had a friend in Dallas, Texas – Nate Levine—and he had a group of small cable television systems and the largest credit collection business in cable television. He believed that with my background I could work with Nate and earn equity in the cable systems I acquired for Nate. I believe that Nate had discussed this with Alan in advance of my meeting with him. When Nate started the collection business, Alan had lent him the money he needed.

Chapter 16

Move to Texas

In late spring, I flew to Dallas to meet with Nate and we quickly came to an agreement. I would work for him, handle marketing, and find cable television systems to acquire. The salary for the marketing function was not much, but the equity I would earn from the acquisitions (i.e., 10 percent) could make a substantial amount of money. This appeared to be a good deal. I'd be developing equity in cable deals without exposing my own money and had a salary to live on. Denise and I moved to Dallas in June of 1983. It was a pleasure to get away from the cold weather. We purchased a house in Plano, Texas. Years earlier, I visited Houston, Texas; it was a lousy trip—hot and humid, the traffic was worse than New York, and I vowed never to return to Texas. I never say never anymore.

Prior to moving, Diane and I had filed for divorce. I can't think of one positive lesson from the divorce. One piece of advice I gave my children was not to rush into marriage. I'm happy to say that my sons James and Bernard were older than I was when they married. They married wonderful women and have built good lives together. Unfortunately, my daughter Marie's marriage ended in divorce. The only thing I was able to do was be with her and try to comfort her, as I knew the pain she was going through.

Working for Nate was easy; he only had twenty-five thousand subscribers. Finding deals was not difficult. Over the years, I had developed contacts in the cable television industry. Within six months, I had lined up an acquisition of a group of cable television systems in the areas around San Angelo and Abilene, Texas. It was a good deal at a good price. It had some upside potential as the existing owner had restricted the channels offered and not constructed into areas he held the franchise for. The deal closed and I waited for the stock to be issued to me. Nothing happened. Finally, I went into Nate's office and asked for the stock to be issued. What happened next is difficult to describe. Picture the scene in the Wizard of Oz when the witch is melting. Nate in almost the same voice as the witch said, "If I give you this, what will be left for me?" He visibly shrank into his chair. Nate's next comment was, "Screw that marketing hat down tight and forget about acquisitions." This was one of the most pathetic sights I'd ever seen. The contrast between Nate and Alan was dramatic. I made more money on Alan's handshake than I was going to make with Nate's contract.

As I stated, Nate's collection business was large; he had contracts with all the major cable television operating companies to handle collection of their bad debts. One of the fellows that worked for Nate in his collections had a similar experience and started a competing collection business. After I left Nate and was in business for myself, I owned and operated many cable systems. As soon as I would take over an operation, I would immediately cancel Nate's collection service. I remember being called by one of Nate's employees asking why we

CHAPTER 16

had canceled the service. My response was, "Tell Nate that Jim said, 'If I pay you all that money for collections, what will be left for me?'"

It really hit me while working for Nate. I'd worked for twenty years for a wide variety of companies. Upon reflecting on my experiences to date, I concluded that I'm glad I did not fit in. I had added value to each company I worked for. One of Uncle Hermie's sayings was, "You take a man's pay, you do the man's job. Make sure you earn him more than he's paying you." After thinking about this for some time, I realized that I really was pretty good at making money for other people. It was now time to make money for myself.

Chapter 17

Starting Out on My Own

One of my favorite passages of the Bible is Ecclesiastes 3:1, "To everything there is a season." I felt that this was my season.

I don't know where I got it from, but one day I listened to a tape, *Think and Grow Rich,* based on the book by Napoleon Hill. The message on the recording made a lifelong impression on me.

The message can be summarized as follows:

1. Everything begins with an idea.
2. Whatever you want to achieve must be built on truth.
3. Fix in your mind your goal. Your goal cannot be vague—be definite.
4. Determine what you are willing to sacrifice to accomplish your goal.
5. Establish a certain date for accomplishing your goal.
6. Create a definite plan for accomplishing your goal.
7. Write out a clear and concise statement of your goal.
8. Be honest about your abilities.
9. Acquire whatever specialized knowledge and/or training is needed.

These nine principles are verbatim from the tape. Denise and I found these words to be powerful and we listened to them over and over again. To this I've added, "You've got to have a dream. If you don't have a dream, how you gonna have a dream come true?" I'd like to take credit for this, but these words come from the song "Happy Talk" in the musical *South Pacific*.

While working for Nate Levine, I investigated many cable television system acquisitions. A group of systems around Lubbock, Texas appeared to have a significant upside potential. I made no secret that I was exploring purchasing the cable television system while I was working for Nate; he suggested if I acquired a system, we could continue to work together. I would do his marketing work, look for more deals, and run my own business on the side. That situation, I knew, could never work, as I had lost all respect for him. This came to an abrupt halt when he found out that I hired Danny Smith, one of his technicians, to work for me. He was really mad. I believe I extracted a small amount of revenge on account of him not keeping his word. As I left his office, I felt elated; this was my day of liberation and the beginning of a grand adventure.

In less than a year I was on my own. I began working from home in March 1985. We had an extra bedroom and I set up an office. After Denise left for the day, I would report to work in our spare bedroom. I approached my workday the same way I did when I was employed. Get up, shave, have some coffee, and go to work. When I wasn't working on elements of the deal, I worked on a correspondence course: "The Cable Television Installer." It was time I found out how a cable television system worked. The purpose of the course is to train new employees how to install and repair the electronics that carry the television signals via cable to a subscriber's home.

CHAPTER 17

For many years, I'd managed many people who worked on the systems. I was great at telling them what to do, but the truth was I had no idea what I was talking about.

I signed a letter of intent to purchase six cable television systems in the Lubbock area. There was one problem; I didn't have the money to pay for them. I committed to purchase the systems serving the communities of Woodrow, Lorenzo, Petersburg, Anton, Buffalo Springs Lake, and Lockney (where the current owners had an office). These cable systems had seventy-four miles of cable plant, passing 3,585 homes, serving 1,426 primary subscribers, and taking 1,047 Pay TV Units. The purchase price was $1,147,000.

All I had was a letter of intent. I knew that I needed to raise the money. While at CI, I had worked closely with John O'Neil, the controller. He was excellent at writing detailed business plans, which I knew I needed to secure financing for the acquisition. I contacted John and asked if he would take my data and assumptions and draft a business plan. I told him I couldn't pay him but would give him 1 percent of the profits when I sold these systems. He agreed and after many lengthy conversations and exchanges of data, he drafted the plan. To close a deal like this requires a lot of legal work. I called Mark Palchick, the former general counsel of CI. He agreed to do my legal work and like John, to be paid when I sold the systems.

Armed with the business plan and letter of intent, I began contacting prospective investors. One day, I called Paul Kagan (a publisher of a cable television finance newsletter) and asked him, "If you were going to finance a cable deal, who would you talk to?" His answer was immediate—"Pete Sokoloff." I called Pete (part owner of Cable Investments), and after a brief discussion, I sent the plan. He spent a week reviewing it and contacted me to make arrangements to meet in Las Vegas at the annual National Cable Television Association (NCTA) Convention.

In the beginning of June, I made arrangements to go to the convention. Mark Palchick was going to be there and agreed to attend the meeting with Pete. Mark and I went to the suite that Cable Investments had at the convention hotel. Cable Investments was a brokerage company and an associate member of the NCTA. The annual convention was a convenient place to network, as it brought people from all over the world together who were associated with the Cable Television industry. We met with Pete Sokoloff, Andy Ishman, John Crowley, and Bob Brown (owner of Cable Investments). We discussed the project, my background, and the opportunities that existed in these under-developed markets. Right away, I told them there was no Hispanic programming, no ESPN, and only one pay TV service on the systems. In the business plan, I had projected the increased revenues to be gained from the services I planned to add and the capital expenditures required to accomplish this. The meeting lasted two hours. They were experienced in the cable television industry, and the questions were comprehensive. As I left the meeting, I knew I had made the sale. Within one week, Pete sent me a draft agreement for financing the acquisition and the creation of a limited partnership that would own the systems. The structure, after some discussion, was that a general partnership formed by me would own 51 percent of the limited partnership and the four investors would own the remaining 49 percent. It was agreed that the losses generated during the startup phase would accrue 90 percent to the four limited partners. This structure was known as tax shelter financing, which was fairly

CHAPTER 17

common at the time—this could not be done under today's tax laws. I am not a good salesman, but I had a good idea and a good plan. Believe in your product, believe in yourself, and people will believe in you.

An observation about the business environment during the middle to late twentieth century: since the end of WWII, the country had experienced virtually full employment. It can be argued that a 4 percent unemployment rate means that, as a country, we are fully employed. Except for short periods, the United States' unemployment rate hovered at around 4 percent. A strange ethos evolved. When you were unemployed, people avoided you as if being unemployed was a contagious disease. During the period of time that I was unemployed, I remember several business acquaintances who saw me at a cable television convention and deliberately walked the other way. I can remember these same people treating me as if I were their great friend when I was a president, vice president, or director. A good way to count your friends is who doesn't walk away when you are unemployed. I'm forever grateful to Mark Palchick and John O'Neil. Another person who never walked away was my father-in-law, Leo Bertholf. In early 1986, Leo and Alice came to visit us. At that time, Denise and I lived in a $150 a month rented house. Leo and I went to have coffee and Leo said, "I've saved up some money, and if you need it you can have it." What he offered was probably every cent he had. I'll never forget it.

At the time of acquisition, the cable systems (Lockney, Woodrow, et. al.) that I acquired generated approximately $330,000 of revenue and $140,000 cash flow. The purchase price was roughly eight times cash flow. Maryland National Bank financed $800,000 towards the acquisitions. The limited partners put up about $150,000 and the former owners got a $200,000 note for the balance. Zero down payments today is common. I'm one of the pioneers of "zero down."

We closed the acquisition in September 1985. Initially, I used the 20 × 20 office, the one used by the former owners. The rent was a hundred dollars per month. The previous owners had a manual billing system. Not much happened with the business during the first six months after closing. I went through three different office girls. I had thought that I could run the systems from Plano, with occasional visits. This was not possible. I began spending my whole week in Lockney while Denise maintained her job in Dallas.

Denise and I were married on November 16, 1985. The wedding ceremony was conducted at our house. I'll never forget how beautiful Denise was; my heart skipped a beat when I saw her in her wedding dress. Being away from her all week was terrible. I had made this mistake once before in my previous marriage and did not want to repeat it.

By the spring of 1986, it was obvious that I could not hope to implement new services without a computerized billing system and competent office help. Denise and I decided that we would move to Lockney, where she would run the office, and we could be together. The added benefit was she could draw a salary. Under the loan agreement, I was not allowed to draw any money out of the business.

Once Denise was running the office in Lockney, we converted to computer billing and began implementing the new services. We conducted customer surveys and asked the customers to vote for what new programming they would like added. Denise and I created all the survey sheets and mail-outs. A converter box was required to receive the new channels. In

CHAPTER 17

each town (except Lockney, where our office was located) we received permission from the city to use City Hall as the location from which to hand out converter boxes to our customers. We sent letters stating that, to receive the new services, our customers needed a converter box and they would have to come to City Hall to pick up the box. This was also a perfect opportunity to sell them the new pay TV services we were offering. This was easy to sell; the city's franchise fees would increase as a result of added revenue. While the customer was picking up the box, Denise would sell them a new pay TV service. We added four new basic channels: ESPN, CNN, etc., (based upon customer preferences). A customer told me that the lights in house windows stayed lit later than ever because of the new services we added. Within six months, we doubled the cash flow.

We had many humorous situations. One customer (a farmer in bib overalls) came in to pick up his converter box. Denise gave him the instructions: a sheet showing the connections needed and a verbal explanation of how to install a converter box. The instructions were to remove the cable wire from the back of the set, screw it into the input of the box, connect the new wire from the output of the box to the TV set, and plug in the converter. He listened carefully and had her go over it twice. In a half hour, he returned with his wife and said, "Explain it to her." Another time, I was told by a customer that he did not like the History Channel because, "everything is old."

Part of our plan to increase revenue in existing areas was by direct door-to-door sales to non-subscribers. I knew little about direct sales. I made up a presentation book and began to go door-to-door selling in the Woodrow area, and Denise accompanied me. She helped refine the presentation, and after a few days, I was able to sell services to 20 percent of the people I contacted. I hired a direct sales person, went over the presentation and turned him loose. The benchmark I used was that he had to sell at least 20 percent of contacts or he would be fired. Anyone that could not sell at least as much as me should not be in sales.

The first salesman I hired was named Tim. I gave Tim a street map showing each house, the sales presentation book, and a ladder. He was able to make the sale and install the new service. I met with Tim every other night. We would review the map to see how many houses he had contacted and go over the new installation work orders and reconcile the money collected. He had to collect the first month's service in advance, and as an incentive to sign up, give the customers free installation. When I got back to the office, we would call the new customer and verify that they were happy with the service. This arrangement lasted with Tim for nearly one year, and in that time, he exceeded my sales-to-contact rate considerably.

When you work for a large company, usually an advertising department handles such work. Running a small business can be a shock—you're the only staff. Denise and I spent many hours designing direct-mail pieces and ad layouts. Luckily, we met Bob Gilliland, owner of Script Printing in Floydada, Texas, who is a talented printer. All of our direct-mail pieces, billing cards, sale handouts, etc., were designed with Bob's help.

The other area we worked on was efficiency. Most cable operators save money on the wrong things. While working for Alan, I found out that he had air conditioning installed in all his trucks. In all the other companies I had worked for, none allowed air conditioning in their trucks, as it cost too much.

CHAPTER 17

I asked Alan about this; his comment was, "No one that has worked service would be without air conditioning. By the end of the day, the servicemen smell terrible and are drained of energy, therefore less productive." He was right.

Another innovation was planned service and installation days. When you have to drive great distances from town to town without a schedule, you'll burn a lot of gas, waste a lot of time, and aggravate your customers. As we added systems and new communities to our company, we sent an introduction letter explaining our service procedures and the customers really appreciated this. With this schedule, we could free up Wednesday, which we used to do preventive maintenance and new construction.

Our computerized billing system was also a welcomed addition. At the time we acquired the Lockney group of systems, the billing was done manually. The customers were given coupon books, an inefficient system that relied on the customer remembering to pay the monthly bill. I was aware of the billing companies in the cable television industry and knew we could not afford their service. I hired a local programmer and designed a billing system. It was a simple system. I met with Bob Gilliland of Script Printing and we designed a computer-generated postcard bill. Recently, Bob and I were talking about this. He remembered when he gave me the quote for the first printing of the new billing cards. He told me the quote and I thought he said seven thousand dollars; Bob chuckled. He thought I was about to have a heart attack—I was beginning to need hearing aids. He realized I had misunderstood him and immediately restated that it was seven hundred. We had a good laugh.

We designed our billing system out of necessity. We could not afford what the large companies were paying to do their customer billing, which at the time cost about fifty cents per bill, plus additional charges for reports on customer activity. The simple system we designed ended up costing about ten cents per bill—a huge savings. This reduced bad debts to one-half of 1 percent, an unheard of feat in the cable television business—a detail thought to be trivial in a large company and therefore overlooked. I heard my Uncle Hermie say, "Pennies make dollars." A few words, but a lot of wisdom.

In all of our acquisitions, we never fired any of the staff; the only one who left was the former owner. When I analyzed a potential acquisition, it was important that there was some element of the business that could be improved and increase profit, otherwise "Why do the deal?" An advantage we had was the cost of the channels we carried. Typically, individual system owners paid a higher price for programming than we did. Our cost for CNN was ten cents per subscriber; an independent owner usually paid fifteen to twenty cents per subscriber. During a launch of a new news channel, CNN offered a contract that froze their rate at ten cents per subscriber for ten years. For some reason few companies took advantage of this offer; we did. Many of the systems we acquired did not have Spanish language programming. We received a large discount from the Spanish networks for being the first to offer their channel in the market.

An interesting note about HBO: there was no consistency in their rates. When I first contacted HBO about a contract, I was put in touch with their regional office in Dallas. They sent me a contract with the standard rate card, which was at least 20 percent more expensive than the large companies were

CHAPTER 17

paying. I protested and their representative said, "That's the rate. Take it or leave it." I asked to speak to his manager. When the manager called, I explained my history of dealings with HBO and asked him if the justice department had ever investigated HBO's discriminatory rates. There is no way HBO could defend volume discounts because their cost of distribution is the same if they have one customer or one million customers. After explaining this to him, we ended up paying the same rate as the largest cable TV operators. To this day, I can't understand why this has never been challenged. I remember the mandatory contributions I had to make to the TelePrompTer PAC (Political Action Committee)—they were the beneficiaries of the discount (volume discount). I'm sure this was just a coincidence.

In June 1986, we acquired the cable system service in Amherst, Texas adding approximately 240 new customers. Maryland National provided the additional financing, as our cash flow had grown sufficient to cover the added debt.

In the fall of 1986, we got the franchise to provide service to the town of Kress, Texas. I didn't think that I could get Maryland National to finance this, so I called up our suppliers and proposed that they allow me six months to pay for the equipment. They did, provided I pay a small interest charge. We built the Kress cable television system in three months and signed up 80 percent of the town in the first month, adding another 150 customers. My son, James, visited while we were building Kress and got firsthand experience building a cable television system. Working new construction turned out to be really fun—the joy of labor is gratifying. We did not have expensive bucket trucks and we had to use hand braces with bits to drill the holes in a telephone pole, but at the end of the day, we could look back at the work and know we had accomplished something.

Denise and I put in long hours. The initial cable subscribers and the next ten thousand customers we added were entered into the billing system by Denise. Sometimes I would help her at night. We had to buy a two-thousand dollar printer one month and that caused major cash problems, but we got through it.

The customers got used to calling at all hours and finding us at work. One woman named Olga from Woodrow, Texas, called at midnight and engaged Denise in a conversation as if it were the middle of the day. As the company grew, we added employees. It was difficult to find people with the aptitude for the work. I noticed that the woman who worked in the restaurant across the street could go through a crowded lunch hour and take the orders without writing them down and never make an error. She was Linda Garcia, one of the most effective people we'd ever hired.

Denise trained Linda to manage the day-to-day operations of the front office. Linda became an expert in our computer operation and supervised our office. As the company grew, Denise worked the marketing and advertising of the new channels being added in the towns. She prepared the advertising for the newspapers and marketing of the upcoming channel additions. She traveled to the towns, handed out converter boxes, and sold the new pay channels. Eventually, she left the company to have our son Patrick, who was born in August of 1990. Linda supervised the customer billing in Lockney and trained the staff in the offices we subsequently opened or acquired. As the company grew, we needed to upgrade the billing system and Linda supervised this project.

CHAPTER 17

On January 1, 1987, we acquired three more cable systems serving Matador, Paducah and Crowell, Texas. In mid-1987, we acquired four additional systems serving Stillwell, Watts, and Westville, Oklahoma, and Lincoln, Arkansas. By this time, we serviced 17 communities totaling 5,270 subscribers. Our annual cash flow (i.e., our annual net income) had grown to $620,000. To put this in perspective, we had increased our customer base 270 percent and our cash flow 340 percent.

We acquired three more cable television systems near Pampa, Texas, serving LeFors, Groom, and Skellytown. The owner of the systems was the widow of the man who had built them. She had a technician named Tim working for her and was concerned that we would fire him. I assured her that we would not terminate him and that we needed qualified technicians. He easily integrated into our operation. After we upgraded the systems, there was not enough service work to keep him busy. We were in the process of rebuilding the system serving Claude, Texas, and we scheduled him to work with Jim Odle and Danny Smith. One day while Jim Odle was in the office, he commented that Tim was faking injuries, trying to establish a disability claim. He also mentioned that Tim thought I was in the Mafia—I guess he thought that Doucette was an Italian name.

I made it a point to observe Tim at work. Typically, I would work with the men when I had time. Unfortunately, the previous owner's faith in Tim was misplaced. I called Tim on a Monday and asked him to meet me at a bowling alley south of Pampa. When Tim showed up, I explained that I was terminating him and explained the reason why. I also said, "Don't you dare file a disability claim—or else!" A disability claim was never filed, and I'm glad Tim never asked, "Or else *what?*" My answer would have been, "Or else, there's not a thing I can do about it!" I thought back to the Uncle Willy "Nice store" episode, and pondered that Texans don't know the difference between French and Italian names.

I continued to look for opportunities to grow the business. To facilitate all the expansion, a new financing arrangement was necessary. The latest batch of acquisitions and the existing debt was financed by Philips Credit. Maryland National continued to hold the original debt. I would identify an area to be constructed or a system to be purchased, Pete Sokoloff would prepare a write-up, and Philips Credit would finance the deal. Our rate of growth was spectacular.

The complexity of the business increased, and that meant we had to develop computerized financial statements and reports for our lenders. For the first few years, we used the computer system of our accounting firm Williams, Rogers, Adair and Company. The partner who handled our account was Don Williams. I engaged Don after we acquired the Lockney group of systems. He had represented the seller and had done a competent job for them. When I engaged Don, I told him, "I don't want you on the other side again." He assisted me in finding an accountant named Brian Cooke, with a warning that "Brian always thinks he's smarter than his boss." As the number of companies grew, we added staff accountants to handle each business. At our peak, we had to produce financial statements for thirteen different partnerships and corporations; two of the corporations were managed companies.

Things went okay with Brian during the first year or so. When talk of the C4 management contract started, I naturally discussed this with him as we would have to add staff and expand our accounting system. For some reason I'll never understand, Brian thought he was the indispensable person. One day he walked into my office and announced that he wanted

CHAPTER 17

a company vehicle, and instead of a salary, he demanded a fee equal to mine for doing the accounting for C4. I was busy and did not think about this proposal because it was preposterous. Over the next several weeks, Brian's attitude struck me as almost funny. When he passed me in the hallway, he would throw his head up and ignore me like a woman in a rage. He even began lobbying Randy Kaufman (an accountant from Don's office), who said, "Jim, you should negotiate with Brian. You need him." I noticed that he'd leave exactly at 5:00 pm. Our staff accountants rarely did. Finally, I told Brian to go home indefinitely and asked Alice Rackley if she would become our chief financial officer/comptroller. She occupied this position until all of the ventures were sold or disposed of. Our financial statements and reports were always timely and accurate. Over the years, she became one of my closest friends.

During the summer of 1988, my son James was between his first and second year of graduate school at Cornell as a finance major. Most grad students had internships during the summer break. The job market was tight and as I had a lot going on, he came to Lockney to work for me as an intern on a number of projects. It was a good summer, but I'm certain that by the time he returned to school, he felt his father was the biggest idiot he'd ever met and that I would shortly go bankrupt. During his last semester of graduate school, James called me. At the beginning of the 1989 spring semester, during his professor's introduction to his senior finance course, he said, "You have spent many years learning about financial theory, but the only thing that matters in business is cash flow," and James blurted out in class, "That's what my father said!" The tuition was worth every cent.

We purchased the system serving Stilwell, Oklahoma, in mid-1988. The service was so bad that many of the customers would not pay their bills. The fellow that had the system built was an accountant from the next town; his son did the service work. Prior to acquisition, I counted the active cable drops; it didn't make sense. There were twice as many active cable television service drops as were represented. (Note: Cable systems were sold at a fixed price per active subscriber.) Two things happened after closing: our technicians balanced the system (i.e., adjusted the gain on the amplifiers to their proper level), and we sent an invoice to every home in town. Customers who had been paying received a postcard bill and all others received a paper invoice in an envelope. As the customers came in with paper invoices to pay their bill, we would verify the services they were receiving, and adjust the bill accordingly. The customers could not believe that we had rebuilt the system in such a short time and said the service was the best they had ever had. When a person came in and said they did not have cable, we would apologize and destroyed the bill. One old Indian fellow came in and said, "The devil sent me this bill," and he lapsed into a chant. It took some time to assure him that the devil had not sent the bill and that it was a computer error. While he was chanting, it started raining; he must have used the wrong chant, otherwise I might have turned into a frog.

There is a concentration of Native Americans in the Stillwell, Oklahoma area. The cable system in Stillwell served a housing development on a Cherokee Indian reservation. As part of my investigation prior to purchasing the system, I knew there were many people receiving cable service who were not paying for it. The reservation had about one hundred homes; of these, only two homes were paying for service. After we purchased the system, I transferred one of our best salesmen (John Harness) to the area. As we had done in the past, we began an audit. The salesman would check each installation against our list of paying customers. When he came across a

CHAPTER 17

home that was receiving service but was not on our list, he would knock on the door. Part of his presentation was that there must be an error in our records as we knew they were receiving service but out records didn't reflect them as a paying customer—surely there was "an error in our records." This approach was very effective; sometimes our records were wrong. The customer usually knew he was getting the service illegally. Our salesman would offer to leave the service connected if the customer would pay for the next month's service in advance. This usually worked well, and we signed up a lot of customers using this approach.

Our salesman, John, caught up with me at our office and told me what happened as he began auditing the Indian Reservation. A note about John: he was one of the most successful salesmen I'd ever known. His approach was something to see; he looked like something the cat dragged in. He wore a very old baseball cap with our company name on it. I tried many times to get him to wear a new hat—no chance. I think I finally convinced him to wash his blue jeans once a week. He was a fellow who most companies would not hire, but his common-man approach was effective and he was a gentle soul. As he began the audit, a man who said he was an officer with the reservation police force stopped him. The officer stated that John was trespassing. After explaining what he was doing, the officer was unmoved and insisted that he leave the reservation or he would be arrested.

I discussed this with Jim Odle, our local manager. It turned out the reservation was served from an amplifier that was located just outside the reservation. Since only two people were paying for the service and almost one hundred homes were receiving free service, I decided that we would disconnect the entire reservation by removing the amplifier. I had this done after 5:00 pm and told the answering service to inform anyone who called that nothing could be done that evening and that they should contact our office. Word travels fast and our office spent the next day signing up "new" customers. We explained to them that to activate the service we needed permission to enter the reservation. It didn't take long for a representative of the tribe to show up. I explained that the permission had to be in writing and have a term that corresponded with the term of our franchise to operate in Stillwell. It was not unusual for cable television companies to have right-of-access agreements and I had one already drafted. I knew the representative was agitated, but he acquiesced and signed the agreement. That settled it—I thought.

The prior owner did not have a background in cable television and made many errors. He had sited the tower in a poor location. After studying the signal strength of the television signals carried on the system, we determined that we could materially improve the quality of the reception by relocating the site. The site was located on the Indian reservation and our plan was to relocate to higher ground not far from our existing site. I contacted the tribal representative, whom I knew from our previous encounter. After I explained what we wanted to do, I was informed that the new location was sacred ground and that the annual lease price would triple, plus we would have to pay five hundred dollars for each tree we removed. I knew he was getting even for the access agreement and effectively told me that.

It did not take long to locate an alternative site. We installed our equipment at the new site and terminated our lease with the reservation. This is a good example of one my uncle's lessons: "The price of greed is high." Now the reservation had 100 percent of nothing, but they had much improved cable television service.

CHAPTER 17

In January 1989, we sold this group of cable TV systems to Mission Cable for $30 million. The decision to sell to Mission was made after Don and I got together. Don recalled that I told the Mission representative I would agree to the sale as long as I received $100 per customer more than they were paying Don for his system in Muleshoe, Texas (Don was a partial owner). In real terms, we got $300 per customer more. At sale, we had 49 cable systems serving 17,324 subscribers. Not a bad day's work. When the sale was complete, I was able to pay Mark Palchick and John O'Neil for their efforts. It is my understanding that Mark was able to pay for the college educations of his three sons with this money.

A number of years later, after James graduated from Cornell with an MBA, he was sent back to Cornell by his employer, Procter and Gamble, to recruit new graduates. One of the résumés he looked at showed that the new graduate had worked for Mission Cable, the company who bought the Cablevision of Texas systems. The interviewee recognized the name and asked if I was his relative, saying that I had put Mission Cable out of business. My son's response was, "My father took the price Mission offered."

One of the points stressed in *Think and Grow Rich* was to set goals. When I moved to Lockney, I established a dollar goal. Not only did I reach my goal, I did it a year early. One thing that I've said to many people is that when you have had a success, savor the moment, for life does not give us many. This moment I savored. After the sale closing with Mission Cable was completed, I followed my uncle's advice: "Shut your mouth, take your money, and go home."

THE NOT SO GREAT AMERICAN NOVEL

Wedding Day, Denise and Me

Me and Danny Smith in front of our first office in Lockney, 1985

Chapter 18

Cablevision of Texas III, Empire Communications, and High Plains Cablevision

We acquired the cable system in Cactus, Texas, in 1989. At the time of acquisition there were about two hundred paying customers. The prior owner had never-ending collection problems. Cactus exists for the sole purpose of providing housing for the workers at the Excel Slaughter Plant, which is 90 percent Hispanic. After the acquisition, we assigned Linda to lead an audit. When the Hispanics heard Linda would be auditing, the world changed. During the audit, we uncovered illegal connections and service problems. Linda explained our billing procedure in Spanish. We also discovered that most of the customers did not have checking accounts, so we set up a collection station at the local grocery store. We added five new Spanish language channels. The Cactus acquisition was a home run; our customer base increased to four hundred. I had a blinding flash of the obvious: Hispanic people will buy HBO when they understand what is being said. Also, the customers found out that there was a new "sheriff" in town named Linda. I've found that with good people, all you have to do is make sure they have the right training, equipment, and let them know what is expected, and you will rarely be disappointed with the outcome.

While the first group of systems was in the process of being sold, a new deal was being assembled. Looking back, it's easy to see that the golden era of cable television was coming to an end. Rumors began about satellite television and other technologies that would compete with the video services offered by cable TV.

My partners at Cable Investments had contacts with Bob Gross, who had assembled a group of systems into a company called Empire Cable. I had known Bob Gross for many years; he had been a marketing person while working for TelePrompTer. Empire Communications was in financial trouble and we believed that I could provide the leadership necessary to correct Empire's problems. Flush from my sale of the initial systems, Philips Credit was willing to finance the acquisition of the Empire systems. We rushed through the closing. I did not inspect the systems and relied on the information provided by Cable Investments who had assured me that, except for some technical difficulties, Empire was a perfect candidate for me to acquire—a mistake! In the closing agreement, Bob Brown had written into the contract that his company, Cable Investments, was to receive a brokerage commission. I did not think this was appropriate but I did not object because they had backed me when I started.

I made a huge error; instead of purchasing assets, we purchased the corporation (i.e., Empire Corporation). The reason, I was told by my partners, for purchasing the corporation was that "it would expedite the transaction." When you purchase assets, you usually have to have the approval of the city council, as they have to reissue the franchise in the name of the

CHAPTER 18

acquiring company. This usually attracts the attention of the community; they would know that a new company would be providing cable television service. In this case, however, in the mind of the customers and the city council, nothing had changed. The poor reputation of Empire carried over.

The former owner had not disclosed what their problems were. I have only myself to blame for not doing the investigation. While the contracts were being negotiated and the debt placement arranged, a competing franchise was being awarded in Chapman, Kansas. After the transaction closed, I became aware of this. I visited the town. I met with several city councilmen and explained that I had recently purchased Empire Communications and that the problems they had been having with the cable television service would be corrected. The prior owner had been aware of this; I had no recourse.

One of the covenants in our loan agreement was that an overbuild (this is an industry term for a second or competing cable system) was reason to call the loan (i.e., an automatic loan default). I explained to the Chapman City Council that having two cable systems was not economically viable. The city council knew this, and their response was that Empire's service was so bad they hoped that our service would lose all its customers and that we would remove our cable television system from the telephone poles. I promised that the service would be improved and that there was new management. To this the councilmen responded, "It's still Empire, and we have heard this before!"

This was a bad situation. While these discussions were going on, we began to reorganize the operation in Kansas. Empire provided service to thirty communities in the northeast quarter of the state.

A city council meeting was called for the purpose of awarding the competing franchise. I engaged John Moore, a former manager of Elmira, New York, for TelePrompTer, now an independent consultant, to attend the meeting with a local attorney. I did this because I felt that Empire needed a new face. John is a southern gentleman with many years of cable television experience. At the meeting, he was not allowed to speak and the council went into "executive session." During this session, the second franchise was awarded. Within two weeks the new system began construction. During the months leading up to this, we had begun upgrading the existing system. There had been many meetings and a lot of local press coverage. This was picked up by Multi Channel News, a cable television trade newspaper. In their article about the overbuild, I was described as a "wildman" by the local competition. I even received a call from Jim Brush, a manager from Adelphia, who told me, "This really looks bad." My comments to Brush do not bear repeating.

I discussed this with Mark Palchick. He researched and discovered that the State of Kansas had a sunshine law (i.e., a franchise cannot be issued in "executive session"). By this time, the competing company was having a difficult time getting customers because our service had improved. I knew that I could not allow this competition to continue. I notified Philips of the loan agreement default and, luckily, they did not call the loan. Some of the other communities Empire served were discussing awarding competing franchises.

I met with the owner of the competing service and offered to purchase his system; he was not interested. It appears that some of the city councilmen were investors in his business. *Well, what to do?* We knew that the awarded franchise could

CHAPTER 18

be challenged and that the competitor's service was not as successful as had been anticipated. Additionally, I had to stop the other communities from taking similar action.

I had Mark draft the lawsuit. I knew that each city councilperson had a million-dollar insurance policy. The League of Cities provided these policies to protect them from litigation resulting from the office they held. We engaged a process server to deliver the lawsuit for $2 million in damages as a result of their issuing an illegal franchise. This was to be delivered on Friday afternoon. I can picture the scene when the councilman arrived home. "Sweetheart, you're being sued for two million dollars. How much insurance do you have?" Within a month, we concluded a deal to purchase the competing system and removed it from the telephone poles.

As part of the reorganization, we opened an office in Minneapolis, Kansas. During the first year, our staff and I spent a substantial amount of time there. Linda Garcia worked around the clock converting the billing system. I spent one month there. The only time I saw Denise was one weekend when she flew to Topeka and we went to the state fair. By this time, we had an excellent technical staff. Our success was directly tied to the competence of the people working with me. The upgrade and reconstruction of the Kansas systems was accomplished by Danny Smith and Todd Town. I underestimated what it would take to accomplish this; it drained the company's money and energy.

We worked closely with the local staff. One day I was in the Minneapolis office and took a call from a customer; she was in tears. I drove to her town, which was thirty miles away, and went to see her. I could not believe the mess our technician had made and he had not repaired her service. I contacted the technician and asked him to meet me at the customer's house. When he arrived, I asked him to explain his actions; he had no answer. I told him that he was terminated and he could find his own way home. I confronted the chief tech with the poor performance of the employee under his supervision and told him that this behavior was unacceptable. His job was to ensure that our customers received the best possible service. One night Danny, Todd, and I were at the motel when we got a call that service in town was off and our answering service was flooded with calls. When we asked who was on stand-by, it was the chief tech, but he was not available. We got in our trucks and went to the town. Danny and Todd restored the service. The next morning, I fired the chief tech. We transferred one of our techs from Texas to fill the position.

This was not the end of the chief tech. He went to the city council and asked to be on the city council agenda so that he could apply for a competing franchise. I attended the council meeting and spoke after he made his presentation. I found out that the former chief tech was also a part-time minister and he played this up in his presentation. By this time, what had happened in Chapman was common knowledge. Luckily, the improvement in our service was noticeable and we had opened an office providing employment to ten local citizens. The council voted seven to zero against the competing franchise. The message was received by the communities we served: Empire was indeed a different company. This was a Pyrrhic victory; a few more victories like this and we would be bankrupt.

The problems in Kansas seemed to be behind us. We needed a manager to oversee the operation. The fellow we hired to handle marketing had done a good job. His name was Roger. I

CHAPTER 18

believed Roger had potential, so I promoted him to manager. After he had been in the job about six months, he had a heart attack and was off work for about three months. His doctor assured me that, given time, he would be able to return to work. During his convalescence, we paid him his full salary and benefits. It was fortunate that we provided health insurance. I was happy when Roger returned to work and, as we had problems elsewhere, I had no desire to return to Kansas and my key people were off handling other Empire problems.

As part of our reporting to our lenders, we had to have our financial statements audited. The loan agreement required that Don William's firm "conduct such investigation as they see fit…" This meant that the accounting firm could randomly select what operations they would visit and perform an in-depth audit. That year, the office selected was Minneapolis. I didn't much think about it. This procedure was followed each year, and since we had spent so much time there, I felt confident that the audit would go smoothly.

As an aside, the loan agreement was written for the benefit of the lenders; the outside auditors were required to read the loan agreement and certify that we were in compliance with all provisions. Naturally, the borrower has to pay for this. When asked to describe this process, I summed it up this way: "It's the lenders saying: *We're going to hang you in the morning. Please bring your own rope.*"

One day I received a call from Scott Alford, the accountant from Don's office that was in charge of the Minneapolis audit. He had uncovered a theft. It appeared that Roger had arranged to pocket some of the installation fees. There was a weakness in our procedure. From time to time, we would offer free installation to any new subscriber. This would last for a fixed period of time. It was easy to change the date on the orders and make it look like the order had been taken during the free installation period. Roger pocketed the cash. After we discussed this, Scott confronted Roger, who admitted that he had done this. Scott estimated the loss to be less than $1,000, as most installations were paid by check. I decided that this was not enough money to bother with a legal action. I talked to Roger via telephone and told him how disappointed I was and that he was terminated. When Don and I talked about this, all Don could say was, "No good deed goes unpunished." I don't like this saying, and put it out of my mind.

Don mentioned that there was a new law firm in Plainview, Texas—"Burgess and Pyles"—and that I should engage them, as they were excellent attorneys. He stated that I would not want them opposing me. As it turned out, I met Randy Pyles and Anita Burgess at a ranch Don was leasing. He had set a date to gather his longhorn cattle and invited me to help. When I got to his ranch, Randy and Anita were busy at work. I joined in and we had a great day. I then made an appointment to visit their office and we discussed them representing my various companies (the bank, cable business, etc.).

It was shortly thereafter that the incident with Roger occurred. As I said, I had put it out of my mind until I was served with a wrongful termination lawsuit by attorneys representing Roger. The area that Burgess and Pyles specialized in was employment law. I called their office and went to see them. At first, I thought this was a joke. Randy and Anita assured me this was no joke and if I did not defend myself, a court could award damages. Any good attorney will advise his client about the cost of the litigation. I said, "Fine, let Roger match me with legal fees and we'll see who cries 'Uncle!'" To

CHAPTER 18

that, Randy pointed out that Roger's attorneys were probably on contingency. "What's that?" I asked. Randy explained that the attorneys would only get paid from the funds they forced me to pay. I'd never heard of this before. Even so, I refused to offer a settlement.

These legal proceedings required that the attorneys had a session with the defendant (me) and ask questions (a deposition). Along with my answers, the plaintiff's attorneys (in this case, Roger's) would use this in preparing for a trial. A date was scheduled for me to be deposed. Roger's attorneys met me at Burgess and Pyles' office. To say the least, I was unhappy. I'll characterize Roger's attorneys' questions:

Attorney: "We'd like you to produce all of your correspondence regarding Roger's termination."

My response: "I have none."

Attorney: "We'd like you to produce any memorandums you've written regarding Roger's termination."

My response: "I do not write memorandums."

Attorney: "We'd like a copy of your employees' procedure manual."

My response: "We don't have one."

In the discussion that followed, I related how Roger had been treated, that I did not need a memorandum or procedure manual to fire someone, and that I did not have to employ someone I did not like—I stopped liking Roger. There are many things that a terminated employee can sue over, but you don't have to employ people you do not like. I've read many instances where employers are forced to pay because of some paragraph in an employee manual or a comment made in a memorandum or letter.

After this meeting, Randy and I had further conversations and we agreed that we should settle this. The cost of going to trial would be $15,000 - $20,000. I think Roger's attorneys initially believed that I would settle this for $100,000. After my deposition, the attorneys realized that there was not going to be a big payday. Randy went to Kansas and settled with Roger's attorneys for $8,500. No matter what, I knew I treated Roger well. At the end of the day, that's all I worry about. You can't control what another person does. I consider Roger one of those stupid people who "doesn't know who their friends are." My Uncle Hermie probably would have said, "You got off cheap."

At the request of my Cable Investments partners, I entered into a joint venture with a man named Bill from the state of Washington. He had approached Cable Investments with a proposal to purchase six cable systems around Spokane, Washington. The deal looked like the first Cablevision of Texas deal. My partners asked me to join a group that would provide the financing and debt guarantees for the purchase. I met with Bill and he appeared to be capable. The first year not much happened, but he was continually late with his subscriber reports and financials. I was busy and did not pay much attention. Also, that first year, the fellows at Cable Investments asked if I would buy them out of the deal because they had had a slow year and needed the money. They had backed me, and the amount of money was not that large, so I bought their interest. Another year went by, and I called Bill to ask him about the business and request that he provide the reports required by the financing agreement. It's a long story—the

CHAPTER 18

result was that Bill had done none of the planned improvements and had, in fact, lost customers. I had a meeting with him and it was obvious that he had no intention of addressing improvements to the systems because he was busy developing other investments.

This was a fine situation. I was the sole guarantor of the debt, which was going to come due within the next several years. I had Bill come to Lockney and informed him that I was going to remove him as general partner and void his equity agreement. Upon his return to Washington State, Bill had his attorney write me. The attorney informed me that the only way Bill's contractual commitments could be terminated was through a civil suit, which I could file in the State of Washington. I engaged an attorney in Seattle and began discussing how to instigate the necessary legal action. What was outlined to me was a procedure that would require continual trips to Washington State. One such trip resulted in Bill not showing for a court appearance. The court rescheduled Bill's appearance for two weeks hence. I went looking for Bill and was told by his office manager that she was directed not to talk to me, and that Bill was not available.

It appeared that Bill had me blocked. I don't remember how Randy and I started discussing this. It was probably on one of our horseback rides. When we rode, we usually talked about things that bothered us. After thinking about this, Randy came up with a strategy. I could sue Bill in Texas because the contracts had been signed in Texas. The suit was filed in federal court and Bill's attorney protested because the business was located in the State of Washington. A hearing date was set and Randy presented my case in federal court. Bill's attorney made his argument. The court agreed with Randy. Now Bill would be required to appear in Texas to defend himself. Within two weeks of the court ruling, Bill's attorney relented and he surrendered his interest in the business. I was free to begin operating the business. I initially sent Jim Odle to Washington to take over the management of the business. It took many years to dispose of the Washington systems at a $250,000 loss. If Randy had not helped me, the loss could have been several million dollars.

(This deal, plus another similar deal in Florida, led to the end of the partnership discussed in Chapter 20, "End of Partnership with Cable Investments." It's interesting to note that when we started out we made a great team—a little success can ruin a partnership.)

One thing I got out of all this is a good friend. Randy and I have had many memorable riding experiences. One trip was with our wives to Cimarron State Park in New Mexico, where we constructed an outdoor shower from tree limbs. We decided not to give up our day jobs, much to the relief of our wives. Our conversations today focus on our children, grandchildren, and what day we'll ride next week.

The Empire systems needed a lot of work. Sometimes our best efforts seemed for naught. In Arizona, we had to construct a two-mile underground line, which had been promised by the previous owner, connecting Eloy to Arizona City. This line was through the desert; I'd been there and helped with the work. We transferred Jim Odle to Arizona to supervise the operation. One day Jim called and said, "The new line is underwater." I couldn't believe it; this was the desert. Apparently, this was in the hundred-year flood plain. This same flood destroyed a one hundred home trailer park where we had just

CHAPTER 18

constructed a new plant to service it. The new line worked perfectly for the two months it was underwater.

There were many problems with the Empire Cable Systems. I was full of myself; a little success and thought I could handle anything. What a lesson. With all the difficulties, there were some accomplishments and humor. Every Empire operation had problems. I was summoned to appear before the city council of Boulder City, Nevada. During the meeting, I was called to task about construction requirements and channel offerings. Our surveys had indicated a desire for the Sci-Fi (Science Fiction) Channel and I committed to offering it. During a break, a young fellow came up to me to thank me for adding this channel. I raised my hand and offered him the Vulcan greeting, "Live long and prosper." To this he responded, "I think I have a friend at the cable company. Can I call you?" "Sure," I responded and quickly rushed back to the council meeting.

Empire had abandoned a tower site five miles out in the desert on a mountaintop and was required to remove it. The council chairman explained that to get to the site, we would have to construct a road, film the process, and restore the desert to its natural state after the site was removed.

Boulder City, Nevada, which is near Las Vegas, was originally built for the workers of the Hoover Dam and had become a favorite retirement destination for Californians. They were really enthralled with the naturalist movement and thought business people represented evil and should be punished whenever possible.

To complete the mountaintop site removal project would cost hundreds of thousands of dollars, which we could ill afford. After some discussion with our local manager, we decided to hire a helicopter to go to the site. We would disassemble the site and have the helicopter, with a sling, lift the pieces to a spot where we could load them onto trucks and take them to a landfill. We set this up like a military operation and in one day removed all of the poles, towers, and buildings without disturbing the desert. When this was complete, I called the city manager to report "mission accomplished" and that the desert had not been disturbed. I knew he was aggravated, as he had delighted in my discomfort at the council meeting.

Shortly after the Empire closing in 1989, I was asked by Walt Cochran, president of Philips Credit, to come to New York. Philips had lent a substantial amount of money to fund a company named C4 Media. What Philips wanted to do was to remove the current owner, as he had defaulted on his loan, and have me manage C4 until such time as the systems could be sold. After reviewing the C4 data, I told Walt that there was no reason why the current management of C4 could not correct their problems. The group of C4 cable systems roughly resembled mine in the size and types of communities they served. I explained to Walt that with some corrections, profitability could be increased, allowing the debt to be serviced.

I heard nothing for six months. I was on vacation in New Jersey when Walt tracked me down. He asked that I meet him in Virginia, at the C4 offices, to begin the process of changing management. One thing I've learned is that when you owe someone as much as I owed Phillips, you do what they ask. The C4 management contract paid a substantial management fee—five percent of revenue.

With the added responsibility of C4, we were roughly managing one hundred cable systems, serving more than sixty thousand customers, spread across eleven states. In addition

CHAPTER 18

to C4 and Empire, I had financed two other cable ventures in Utah and Florida. We also managed another distressed group of cable systems for a bank that was located in Florida, not far from the system I was financing. We were busy. Our Lockney office now employed seventeen people. This office controlled the customer billing and did all the accounting. Each month our office prepared reports for the two managed companies, our own systems, and two self-financed operations. We were operating ten partnerships and corporations. We had offices from Florida to the state of Washington.

In the middle of this swirl of activity was Alice Rackley. If you ever met Alice, you'd think, *This is a sweet Sunday school teacher*, which she is. Remember it's not the size of the dog in the fight, but the size of the fight in the dog. I don't think we ever missed a reporting deadline. Don't cross Alice.

Chapter 19

Diversification, The IRS, and Politics

I was twice audited by the IRS. At the beginning of one audit, Don Williams called me with an offer from the IRS auditor; "Give me a check for ten thousand dollars, and I'll leave." My response was, "No!" About three months into the audit, Don called me and told me that it had just been discovered that a charitable contribution had been missed when our return was prepared. Instead of paying ten thousand dollars, I received a refund of ten thousand dollars. I repeat the numbers because these were the exact amounts.

Don knew the tax laws better than the IRS auditors. As I had purchased a ranch and a farm, I also qualified as a farmer. One day, Mary Allenson, who worked for me as a staff accountant, came into my office and said, "You're in trouble." I asked "Why is that?" She responded, "The IRS doesn't believe you are a farmer." I think I laughed for five minutes. Mary was aghast, but I told her not to worry, as farming represented less than 1 percent of our earnings.

Mary did not know that prior to the sale of Cablevision of Texas I and II, Don devised a merger of the "C" corporation I had initially formed to operate the cable business into a new partnership. Don explained if we did not liquidate the corporation, we would have to pay a double tax, corporate tax, and individual tax, but Congress had inserted into the law a section dealing with this issue. He explained that his approach was not bulletproof, as the IRS statute could be interpreted differently. I called Don and told him to surrender to the IRS, as I was not a farmer. Don said, "No, under the IRS code, you qualify as a farmer," and that he would continue to fight. When the audit was complete, it was determined that I was indeed a farmer. The merger was never challenged.

The Internal Revenue Code is too complicated. When I took the federal tax course at Pace College, the professor stated, "Don't look for logic in the code; its purpose is to raise money to support our government." This simple reason for the code has been lost.

When Ronald Reagan ran for President, one plank of his program was simplification of the tax code. During his administration, he accomplished his goal; Congress passed and he signed the Tax Simplification Act, all 1,700 pages of it. One person who does comprehend the tax law is Don Williams. He graduated from Texas Tech with a straight-A average and passed the CPA exam with one of the highest grades ever recorded. The IRS agents are no match for him. While I do applaud Don's ability, I dislike that our taxing system has gone far afield from its purpose. The laws are written to grant special favors for the wealthy. My personal experience, described above, is a good example. By writing ambiguous statutes, our wealthy citizens are legally allowed to avoid taxes. This ambiguity is not available to our hard-working citizens who file the standard 1040 return.

CHAPTER 19

A note about politics: Throughout my career, I've had many contacts with the federal government. My first was when I got the job at the Board of Elections (BOE) in 1962. Adelphia Business School arranged the interview with the BOE for a position as IBM machine operator, they offered me a job, and I accepted. I was informed that I had to be a member of a political party. The interviewer told me I'd have to be a Democrat. I did not know what a Democrat was, but I needed the job so I agreed. We were settling on the start date of my employment when the interviewer realized that he had made a mistake and said that I'd have to be a Republican. After wrestling with this for two seconds, I agreed—sometimes when you need a job, you'll agree to anything.

I had to go to the local Republican Party Club in my neighborhood and join, which I did. The club was run by Benjamin Westervelt. He had been the leader of this club for many years and also worked for the BOE. In the BOE, each job function has two people, one from each party. When the mayor of New York was a Democrat, the head of the BOE was a Democrat, the assistant a Republican. If a Republican was elected subsequently, they would switch jobs. The day I was hired, they also hired a Democrat IBM machine operator. He and I joked about this. There were two other redundant positions in registration; one entered into the log the names of eligible voters, the other person removed the names of voters who died. I don't remember if they switched jobs when the party of the mayor changed... something to ponder.

In my brief time at the BOE, there was a mayoral election. I was informed that I had to "volunteer" to work for the campaign. The Republican candidate was Louis Lefkowitz, the then current comptroller of the city. We had to go door-to-door soliciting support for Louis. The club was located in a predominantly Italian neighborhood. While today it is not politically correct to mention ethnic differences, at that time that was not the case. A typical reaction at the door was, "What kind of a name is Lefkowitz?" Obviously, he was Jewish. That was a tough sell, but I tried. Mr. Lefkowitz lost by a landslide. At the club, the old timers said they knew he'd never be elected. This raises the question as to why I had to put in so much of my own time in a losing effort. The answer was, "You do this to keep your job." I wonder …is this what Thomas Jefferson had in mind when he drafted the US Constitution?

Many years later, after I was established in Lockney, Don Marble, with whom I was partnering on some cattle, convinced me that I should contribute to the campaign of our local congressman, Bill Sarpalius. With some reluctance, I agreed. Over the next two election cycles, I got to know the congressman. During one of his campaign swings, he stayed at our house. I felt honored to host a member of Congress. Bill invited Denise and me to his wedding. We traveled to Washington, D.C., and he was married in a room in the U.S. Capitol. We were impressed.

The congressman told me that if I were ever in Washington, D.C., to let him know and we would go to dinner. My attorneys had their offices in D.C., so I took him up on his offer. We had a nice dinner. What I discovered is that Bill rarely discussed substantive issues with his constituents; this was the job of his staff. There was a staff person stationed in Lubbock, Texas, who would visit our area, usually every six months, and would stop by my office for a chat. We would discuss whatever issues were being worked on in Congress. During one meeting I was told, "The new tax bill will really help you." This

CHAPTER 19

struck me wrong and I explained, "The congressman has a lot of people to worry about; Jim Doucette is not one of them. Take care of my customers and I'll do fine." He was taken aback by this. I further explained that I measure the congressman's performance by how he takes care of the least of our people. During my dinner with Bill I repeated this; he seemed to appreciate this advice.

At that time there was a bill in Congress to impose strict regulation on the cable television industry. Al Gore was now Vice President and was still on the campaign to punish cable TV companies for the issue I mentioned earlier. Just prior to the vote in Congress, the congressman's aide called me. We chatted a while and he finally got around to why he called. He stated the new telecommunications bill was going to be voted on the next day. I was well aware of that; it would impose requirements on my business that would cost me a lot of money and the bill was badly flawed. He went on to say that the congressman knew I was in the cable television business and that was why I was being called. Then he stated that the congressman was going to vote for the bill.

I asked the aide, "Have you had complaints about my company?" He responded, "No, your company has an excellent reputation." I asked, "Have you had complaints about Cox Cable or TCA (the only other cable television companies in this congressional district)?" His response was, "No." I said, "Then tell me why the congressman is voting for the bill." He explained that the congressman said, "I have to go along with the administration on this bill." I'm certain that Thomas Jefferson never intended for our elected officials to "go along" to the detriment of their constituents. Needless to say, that was the last contribution I ever made to the congressman's campaign. The next election, Bill Sarpalius was voted out of office.

I saw that aide a number of years later when he was running for Congress and reminded him that if he were elected, his job was to represent his district, not to "go along with the administration." He did not win the election, so I'll never know if he listened to my advice.

Chapter 20

The End of Partnership With Cable Investments

In the early 1990s, my relationship with my partners began to deteriorate. We had an investor/lender party in Breckenridge, Colorado, at a very expensive resort, which I was paying for. Bob Brown acted as if it was his weekend. At the party, Don Williams noticed how freely Bob was sending back hundred-dollar bottles of wine that I was paying for. Bob did acknowledge that, through my brilliance, we had all made a lot of money. After this remark, I noted to Don, "In a rising market, everyone's a genius."

I read an interview that Bob Brown gave to a reporter from an industry publication (Multi Channel News). He talked as if he managed Cablevision of Texas and referred to the people in Lockney as "his" staff. At first, I didn't think much of it. As it turned out, Bob made commitments that I was expected to fulfill; he and Pete Sokoloff had begun franchising the Island of Aruba. The group of us visited Aruba: Denise and I, Pete Sokoloff, his wife, and a consultant Pete had hired to open the political doors for us there. As we toured the island with a local government official, two things struck me: this would be a monumental construction project, and we would have to hire anyone the government told us to. Our consultant said this was how payoffs are handled on the island. This consultant had an arrangement to provide cable television service to Czech Republic. I wondered how many Czechs I'd have to hire. He had committed to purchase a cellular telephone license for the north section of Las Vegas and had planned to purchase the cable system serving West Yellowstone, Montana. The actual work would be done by the "Lockney staff." This came to a head in 1995. After much discussion, it was decided that it was time for the partnership to end. We ended up trading my interest in the above-mentioned deals for their interest in Cablevision of Texas/Empire.

In 1997, Philips Credit called me and said they had a buyer for C4: Adelphia Communications, a name from my past. The management contract with C4 had been very good to us. It was time to sell. Philips had no idea of my past association with Adelphia. I believed that selling C4 was in Philips' best interest, so I placed a call to John Rigas. He did not accept or return my call.

As part of buying any cable operations, it is a good practice to inspect the cable systems (i.e., due diligence), and to visit with the local elected officials to discuss the franchise transfer. This process can be expensive. Not having heard from John didn't bother me, as it was widely known that his sons were running the business. Adelphia had grown to more than one million customers nationwide. From our local managers, I had heard that the Adelphia people had made some comments that "this guy in Texas is draining the money out of the local community, but this will stop when Adelphia takes over."

One Friday, I received a call from my loan officer at Philips, Morey Halfon. He said that the Adelphia people had reviewed

CHAPTER 20

C4's financial statements and that "no one could honestly make that much money in cable television." I contacted Don Williams and Tim Kelley (my attorney) and asked them to meet me at the Philips office in Manhattan on Monday for a meeting with Walt Cochran (president of Philips Credit). We arrived at 9:00 am and after a short discussion with Morey, I stated that Don and Tim knew my business intimately and if he had any questions about my honesty, he should ask them. I further stated that "neither of these people makes enough money off me to cheat." I left the office. Within five minutes I was summoned; I never heard another comment about Adelphia's claim. The Adelphia people did not know that I had passed my low rates for cable programming (i.e., we had a 10-year deal for CNN at ten cents per customer) to C4, and that our billing cost per subscriber was ten cents per customer, per month, versus the industry average of fifty cents. The Adelphia people asked to see the programming contracts; I could not show them to them because the contracts had a non-disclosure clause.

We discussed that Adelphia was trying to negotiate the price down and that they had a history of underhanded business practices. The price had started at $44 million; Philips had agreed to reduce the price to $42 million. After a short discussion, we agreed to look for other buyers. Within two weeks, we had another offer for $48 million and C4 was sold. If John Rigas had returned my call, things might have been different. The day the C4 deal fell through, two people knew what happened—John Rigas and me. About a year later, I saw John at a trade show. He asked me, "Are we even yet?"

During negotiations of the sale of C4, I was involved in a conference call with the purchaser, his attorney, and a number of Philips executives. After the introduction, one fellow (I'll call him "Mr. Important") said to me, "I remember you standing outside of John Malone's, president of TCA Corp., with your hat in your hand." I said, "You're mistaken. I've never been to Malone's office." "Oh, yes, it was you," he retorted with a defiant air of certainty. I believe he had me confused with Bob Brown (one of the investors in Cablevision of Texas). As this had nothing to do with closing the C4 transaction, I let it pass.

After the C4 transaction was complete, I received a call from Don Williams who said that the buyer needed me to sign an affidavit attesting to the accuracy of the C4 financial statements. The new company needed this to complete a filing with the Security Exchange Commission so that they could register stock for an initial public offering. I told Don, "I am not required to do this, and further, this fellow had gone out of his way to insult me." I promptly forgot about the conversation.

A few weeks passed and Don called me again stating, "You have to sign the affidavit as it is holding up their filing." My response: "That's not my problem and I have no desire to help this rude individual." I explained what had happened and that Mr. Important didn't even have the courtesy to call me as he probably felt that was below him.

After some discussion, I told Don that if they wanted this affidavit signed, it would cost them fifty thousand dollars. About two days later, Mr. Important called me. He prefaced the conversation by saying, "I heard about your demand for signing the affidavit, but I have to hear it for myself." He asked me how I had arrived at the fifty thousand dollar fee. I explained, "This is the amount I need to purchase a new Lexus for my wife." He thought that confronting me would make a difference.

CHAPTER 20

After explaining how he had insulted me, I told him, "Further, the affidavit will not be signed until such time as my attorney, Tim Kelly, has the money in his escrow account to be paid to me when Tim delivers my affidavit to you." I further explained, "I don't need the money, but I wanted to teach (Mr. Important) a lesson to treat everyone with respect." The money was paid the next day. I've heard Don tell this story many times, "Jim's rate of pay is fifty thousand per hour, and he gets it."

Within a couple of years, John Rigas and one of his sons were in jail for misappropriation of $100 million of corporate funds. After the sentences were handed down, Frank Cooper called and said, "Jimmy, I hear your old partner is in the clink." I responded, "When I worked at Adelphia, John Rigas's sons used to come into the office and play with the adding machines--I didn't think it was a good idea then." One son was not convicted in the trial, as he was said to be "too stupid to know what was going on"—that son was a graduate of Harvard Law School. John Rigas, for his part, received a fifteen-year sentence, in effect, life, as he was 79 years old when the sentence was given. The lenders hired a group of professional managers to liquidate Adelphia. It is my understanding that John Rigas's share of the proceeds was $1.5 billion. As Uncle Hermie would say, "He stepped over a dollar to pick up a dime."

My son James also called to say he remembered swimming in John Rigas' pool, and that he remembered us moving back to New York, but never knew the reason. I explained what had happened while I worked for Adelphia. I think he appreciated hearing the story. During this same visit to John's, my son Bernard almost drowned. John's wife, Doris, jumped into the pool to save him. I wish someone had saved John from his greed; this brave lady will spend the twilight of her life alone.

We operated the C4 cable systems for about five years. I'm not 100 percent certain of the dates when things changed at Philips Credit. As I understand it, Philips N.V. (the parent company of Philips Credit) decided that they no longer wanted to be in the finance business. The president of Philips Credit was fired, right after the C4 sale. The person brought in to replace him was a fellow named Chris Cundy, a career Philips Finance executive. In September of 1996, Mr. Cundy asked if I'd come to New York to visit with him. We went to lunch and Chris began the discussion. He told me that Philips wanted to exit the credit business and that he might have to ask me to throw the "keys" on the table. I did not react. I thought the job I had done for Philips on C4 and the fact that my loan payments were up to date should have earned me some forbearance. The off-hand manner of Cundy's remarks was offensive. In reality, this was good timing. With the introduction of Direct TV, the sale price of cable television systems dropped. Based on the price per subscriber that was being paid, it didn't seem possible to recoup my money and Philips would also take a loss.

I did make an effort to move the loan to another lending company, to no avail. It was clear that the glory days of cable TV were over. Early in 1997, Chris Cundy came to Lockney to visit. We met at Don Williams' office; Chris reiterated Philips' desire to exit cable lending. I pointed out that this was Philips' problem, not mine. It would be difficult to force liquidation since our loans were performing. We went back and forth. Cundy finally asked what it would take to get me to agree to the sale of the cable television systems financed by Philips. I

CHAPTER 20

told him, "One million dollars." Don and I exited the office so Chris could telephone whomever he had to. Upon returning, he told us Philips had agreed. After Chris left, Don gave me a high five. I know that Chris was the bearer of the news and does not deserve criticism. What I can criticize is that Philips had no basis for treating me the way it did. I had worked hard to maximize the amount they realized on the C4 transaction and paid them what we owed. Within a short period of time, I would wrap up all my cable operations and retire. It took about a year to dispose of the cable systems financed by Philips and by the end of that year, Philips fired Chris Cundy.

An interesting insight into the cable industry occurred to me during a cruise Denise and I went on in 2009. When we registered on board, I noticed that there were many Comcast employees taking the cruise. I had heard of Ralph Roberts, the founder of Comcast; he has a great reputation. One night Denise and I were playing blackjack. I witnessed a Comcast executive laboring over whether he should hit a soft six. For the non-gamblers reading this, the object in blackjack is to get as close to twenty-one without going over, in which case you automatically lose. Also, you have to be closer to twenty-one than the dealer. A soft six is an ace and a five, which can either be six or sixteen, as an ace can be counted as eleven or one. A sixteen is usually a losing hand because the dealer has to take another card if he has less than seventeen and must hold on seventeen. There is no way to break a soft six; the only thing you can do is improve your hand and your chance of winning. Anyone playing blackjack who can't understand this should not be playing. The Comcast executive could not figure this out.

The cable television industry never attracted great thinkers. Mostly the industry attracted people like me; hard workers without Ivy League educations or those like the Comcast executive. One night the fellow asked me what my name was, and when I told him, he said, "I've heard of you." I responded, "You have me confused with someone else." If I had had any Comcast stock, I would have immediately sold it (someone who can't figure out blackjack is someone I don't want running my money). It's not surprising that he knew of me, as I had previously worked with many of the current Comcast executives. It's really a small industry. (Note: Comcast is doing very well. Ralph's son Brian, who is now Chairman and CEO of Comcast, graduated from the Wharton School of Business. Comcast is diversifying out of cable television. I hope they never venture into gambling.)

Chapter 21

First National Bank of Lockney

In 1990, Don Williams discussed my financial situation. One observation that Don made was that I had all my wealth concentrated in cable television. I don't remember how I heard this, but it came to my attention that the Lockney bank was for sale. It didn't take long to conclude a deal to purchase the bank. The purchase price (i.e., market price) for a bank had dropped dramatically because of the savings and loan scandal; banks were selling below "book value." I also purchased a burglar alarm company, First Alert, a telephone installation company, and invested with a local group to build a horse racetrack. Two fellows I knew from the Ford Bank Group had acquired a trucking company and I invested in it. We were also very busy in the early 1990s in acquiring the rights to construct cable systems in California and the state of Washington.

One day, Don Williams asked me how I slept at night owing so much money. I responded, "It's not me that has to worry; it's the people who lent me the money that have to worry." I've heard Don repeat this story many times.

Before this transpired, while I was negotiating with Jim Strange (no relation to the Stranges later mentioned) for the purchase of the Amherst cable systems, I had a conversation with Kim King, President of First National Bank of Lockney. Kim stated that he was sorry to lose the loan that the bank had made to the former owners of the Lockney cable television system. When I purchased the system, part of the settlement was that the former owners pay off all of the debts and liens (which include loans and all other encumbrances to the title) on the cable system. When I completed the business plan for the acquisition of the Amherst system, I took it to Kim and prepared a loan application for the money needed to purchase the system. After about a week, Kim called me and stated, "I've got good news and bad news on your loan. The good news is that the answer is quick. The bad news is that it is no." I was tempted to tell him that it was *he* that asked *me* to apply for the loan, but I knew I could place the loan with my existing lender. I really think Kim was quite pleased with himself turning down my loan request. People that use this good news/bad news method of delivering bad news sometimes seem to derive pleasure from the discomfort of the recipient.

Being a small town, everyone knew what happened. By this time, I had made several friends in town, and they commented that Kim King was well known as a "butthead." Ironically, in 1990 as I stated, I had purchased the bank. Luckily, Kim King had already left the bank. I know he knew I purchased the bank. The reasons for purchasing the bank had nothing to do with revenge, but I do enjoy turning the tables on "buttheads." It became a local joke that it's not a good idea to cross Jim Doucette.

As I mentioned, when we acquired the First National Bank of Lockney in 1990, the prices were low due to the savings and loan scandal of the 1980s. This was similar to the financial

CHAPTER 21

meltdown of 2008, on a smaller scale. The savings and loan industry had over-leveraged their real estate loans throughout the 1970s and '80s. When housing prices retreated in the 1980s, their loan portfolios were not sustainable and because they had federal insurance, it required the U.S. taxpayer to bail them out. This led to a series of liquidations and reduced the value of all banks. I purchased the bank for three-quarters of book value (i.e., net equity), an extraordinarily low price.

During the nine years we owned the bank, we never forced a customer into bankruptcy. One customer we knew had a couple of bad years back to back. Our loan committee discussed a plan that would allow this customer to recapitalize his loans and continue in business. A number of times I asked Ronnie Hardin, president of First National Bank of Lockney, if the customer had been in to discuss his loan. He assured me that it was just a matter of time, that the customer would be in and the loan would be restructured. To Ronnie's surprise and disappointment, the customer filed bankruptcy. After going through the bankruptcy court, a plan was made to liquidate his farm and restructure the loan. The restructured loan was the same as we had prepared in advance. The difference was the customer lost his farm and was fifteen thousand dollars poorer—another case of someone not knowing who his friends are.

At the time of acquisition, the bank didn't have any Hispanic employees. This seemed incredible to me; Hispanics make up 60 percent of the population of Lockney. I discussed this with Ronnie and told him I thought it would be a good idea to hire a Hispanic. Within six months, there was an opening; a non-Hispanic individual was immediately hired as the replacement. Finally, I told Ronnie that the next person hired would be a Hispanic; I know he was not to happy, but our next hire was Hispanic.

The bank did not offer health insurance to its employees, only the officers. I was struck by the inequity of this and added all employees to the health plan. We had instituted a self-insured plan that meant that we would fund the coverage directly and use an insurance management company to process claims. When unusual claims were made, I would be asked to rule on them. One claim was for fertility treatments. Great proposal. Pay for the employee to get pregnant and pay to have the child delivered. As it turned out, the young lady got pregnant with no help from the bank, had her baby, which we paid for, and promptly resigned. Another tried to have his wife's birth control pills paid for by the bank. There are some things I don't feel are the employer's responsibility. This is an example of people getting lucky (getting coverage they never had), and then getting greedy. This thought is my own, but I think my uncles would agree.

In 1990 and 1991, I was awarded franchises to build cable television systems in the Texas communities of Quitaque, Turkey, Nazareth, Adrian, Hartley and Channing, as well as San Jon, New Mexico, and acquired the cable systems in Cactus, Etter, Miami, and Wheeler, Texas. We negotiated a loan with Norwest Bank for the construction and acquisitions. Norwest Bank had recently acquired banks owned by the Ford Bank Group in and around Lubbock, Texas. I had purchased the Lockney Bank from executives of the Ford Bank Group who owned the Lockney Bank privately outside of the Ford Bank Group. Within a year, all of the Ford Bank Group executives left Norwest. Immediately, they formed a bank holding company titled State National Bank, and began

CHAPTER 21

acquiring banks in the same communities served by Norwest. I was approached and asked if I would like to invest in the new venture, so I did. The fellow in charge of correspondent banking for Norwest came to visit me. He informed me that they were not happy that I invested in State National, as they were the Lockney Banks' correspondent bank. Smaller banks needed to have a correspondent to handle Federal Reserve transactions; the Ford Bank Group had performed this function prior to being sold to Norwest. I asked him why Norwest didn't get a non-compete agreement (i.e., they can't go across the street and open a business to compete with you) as part of the purchase price for the Ford Bank Group; he became agitated. I explained to him that our bank was growing and that the key to our success was our community bankers. The State National Group was recruiting from all the local banks; I, being a stockholder, automatically put my employees off the list of potential recruits. (The major asset in banking is your loan officers, they make the cash register ring; without them, you don't have a business.) He did not understand this. I asked him if he'd ever seen *The Godfather*, to which he responded, "No." I suggested he see it and told him some of the Godfather's wisdom: "Keep your friends close and your enemies closer." (The threat they posed was reduced by my investment in them.) To this, all I got was a blank stare and a threat to cancel our correspondent agreement. After he left the office, I immediately began calling area banks. We eventually moved our correspondent business and High Plains loans to Amarillo National Bank. Not too many years later the Norwest Bank was liquidated. None of our community bankers were recruited by State National Bank.

One thing that soured me on Ronnie occurred when I was trying to raise some cash locally. I quickly found out that there existed a "good old boy" network with the local bankers. Ronnie must have heard of my discussions with area banks. As part of Ronnie's compensation package, I had set up a plan that allowed him to purchase 10 percent of the bank at below cost, based on his performance. Ronnie came to see me and proposed that he would help me and purchase his stock, but I would have to take a discount on the already discounted price. I was tempted to throw him out of the office, but instead I just declined his offer.

Denise and I owned The First National Bank of Lockney for about nine years. During that time, we increased the bank's assets from $19 million to $90 million. After the initial acquisition, we acquired banks in Olton, Silverton, and Paducah, Texas, and opened a new branch in Floydada, Texas. On the day the Floydada branch was opened, August 12, 1990, our son Patrick was born in Lockney. I missed the grand opening.

I enjoyed the bank, but I could tell I was losing my enthusiasm. I remember saying to myself, "Oh crap, it's Thursday and I have another loan meeting." This was in 1998. One thing convinced me it was time to sell: the Glass Steagall Act was going to be repealed. In my opinion, this was one of the major causes of the 2008 recession. With the repeal of the act, bankers would be allowed to enter the brokerage and insurance business (risky business), and the constraints on purchasing securities with bank funds was relaxed. The bankers knew that banking was getting ready for unprecedented profits. Immediately the value of banks skyrocketed. I knew I had an opportunity to make a substantial profit on the First National Bank of Lockney. These opportunities come and go—you

CHAPTER 21

have to seize the moment. Eight years later, you couldn't sell a bank. A piece of advice from Uncle Hermie many years ago: "Always sell into a rising market."

I went to a meeting about bank valuation. At this meeting, several brokers gave presentations about what an owner could expect to make if they sold their bank, given the current valuation. One fellow gave a presentation about how he could guarantee top price and would charge five percent of the purchase price—too much! I contacted a firm that prepared sales brochures for banks for a fixed fee. I had brochures sent to three local banks. The first to respond was City Bank Lubbock. They contacted me and set up a meeting at their office.

The only people at the meeting were Mike Liner, president of City Bank, Curtis Ford, chairman of the board and principal owner, and me. Mike made several attempts to lower my price expectations. Finally, I said to Curtis, "Take a blank piece of paper and write down the amount you think First National Bank of Lockney is worth," and I said that I would do the same. Next, I asked that we both turn over the piece of paper at the same time. Our prices were four percent apart. We discussed this for a few minutes and agreed on my price, I would hold a note for five years for 80 percent of the price at two percent below prime rate.

The day we closed the sale of the bank, I arrived at the closing about thirty minutes late, deliberately. I walked into a conference room to find four or five City Bank executives being given a lesson by Don Williams on how you close a transaction. I've been through many deal closings. It was typical for a purchaser to try to lower the price at the last minute; I had done this many times. Don could negotiate, but could not come to a final agreement without me being present at the meeting. Curtis Ford was there, he had no excuse. The City Bank people made an error by having a blackboard in the room. I'd learned many years earlier, you never give "Professor Williams" a blackboard. Extremely bright, he would lecture at length. The list of last-minute adjustments they had was forgotten, and they were happy to pay me and end their torture. When I walked into the room, I commented privately to Don, "It looks like you've got them surrounded."

After the closing was completed, Curtis Ford gave me a bronze sculpture called *Changing Outfits* with the inscription: "To Jim Doucette, a Man of His Word."

At the closing of the sale of the banks, Ronnie received the largest check he'd ever received in his life. He did not say thank you or offer to shake my hand. What he did not know was that I could have changed his payment from ordinary income to capital gains with a stroke of a pen, reducing his tax rate from 50 percent to 10 percent. Ronnie found out what it was like to take a discount.

The day after closing I went over to Don Williams' office and gave him a check as a bonus for the excellent job he had done. Sometimes you have to do more than say thank you.

Chapter 22

Time to Retire

I'm reminded of a Kenny Rogers song that basically says, "You've got to know when to hold 'em, know when to fold 'em." Stated another way, "If you stay too late at the party, the only girls left are the ugly ones."

By the end of 1998, I had sold off most of my businesses but I still owned the burglar alarm business and twenty small cable systems. After discussing this with Todd Town, he decided he and Scott Alford would purchase the burglar alarm business. I made them a ten-year deal and they purchased First Alarm. I'm happy to say they paid the note off and have gone on to build a successful business. Over the years, I've kept up with Todd and marvel at his success. A number of years ago I stopped in his office in Amarillo and asked to see Todd. The lady asked who I was; I told her I was Jim Doucette. Her comment was, "So you're the Jim Doucette we've heard so much about." During one conversation, Todd asked me, "After all the years I worked for you, do you know what I've learned?" I had to tell him I had no idea. His response was, "You have to show up every day." This was an insight I'd never thought about, but it is so true. The first ingredient in success is *you have to be there.* I tried to think if I'd ever taken a sick day—I can't remember one. It is gratifying to hear of someone else's success and know you had a part in it.

There were approximately twenty cable systems, half in Texas (High Plains Cable) and half around Spokane, Washington (Elk River Cable) that no one wanted as they were in really small towns. I told Jim Odle and Dave McGraw that I was ready to retire and getting out of the business and that if they wanted, I would set up a financing structure that would allow them to purchase the systems in their respective areas. With the advent of Direct TV, the need for cable was going away. One thing that had a profit potential was Internet access. The cable systems provided a perfect platform for this. In 1999 (roughly), we contracted with them to purchase the systems in their areas.

After the transfers were complete, Jim and Dave called to say they were going to attend a Cable TV Convention and had appointments to visit with Internet access equipment suppliers. I said, "That's great." Their response was, "You always handled these details." I responded, "That's true, but you now own the business and it's time you handled this. Enjoy the convention. Goodbye, and good luck." A week later, they called and asked if I would attend the convention with them. We went together to meet with all the vendors and concluded arrangements to implement the new Internet access service. I was happy to help.

When Internet access was being installed in Miami, Texas, Jim Odle called me and asked if I'd like to watch the new service installation. The head end site in Miami overlooks a beautiful valley. I met Jim and we drove up to the site. An old fellow was digging the footers for the dish. He looked familiar,

CHAPTER 22

and I realized that he was the former president of Sammons Communications. After we exchanged greetings he told me what had happened. The owners of Sammons sold the company out from under him and he did not receive a cent. I thought, *"There, but for the grace of God, go I."*

Unfortunately, Jim Odle did not have it in him to operate a business on his own and I had to make another agreement for Dave McGraw to take over the Texas systems. Dave was not able to completely pay off the notes; he did the best he could. In 2007, I told Dave, "It's time to sell the Internet access customers and move on." I've enjoyed working with Dave and he is now the county commissioner where he lives and will probably stay in politics. Once when he and I were talking, I mentioned that some people were meant to sign the back of the check and some were meant to sign the front. Apparently, he used this line in a local political debate and it made the local news. Dave was elected.

This story brings me back to a series of meetings I had with Joe Hipple. When I was with TelePrompTer, Joe reported to me. He was the manager of the Islip, New York, cable system. He was a good manager with a can-do attitude. Joe called me in 1992 and asked if he could visit me. When he arrived, he stated, "I want to do what you have done—purchase a cable system and make a lot of money." He had his eye on building a cable system in Aleato, Texas (a suburb of Fort Worth). We spent time going over my original business plan and planned to meet again when his plan was completed. In about a month he came to Lockney again and I reviewed his plan. The plan was well prepared, but I questioned him on one item. He had written in a salary of sixty thousand dollars a year for a manager. When asked who this was, he stated, "It's my salary." I explained that this would never work. He replied, "They've got to understand that I need this to live on." I told him that the financial community will not pay when you first start out, and that you only make money after the lenders are paid. Joe's response was, "You mean I have to work for nothing?" I also pointed out that he would have to pledge any assets he had as collateral for the loans required to finance his venture. This floored Joe. He never realized what was required. He had the desire, but when confronted with what was required, he was unwilling to do it. I know that Joe ended up working for another company. The point is, if you want to be in business for yourself it takes more than desire. The test of your resolve is to ask yourself: "What am I prepared to sacrifice to achieve my dream?" and you have to have absolute confidence in your ability to do what is necessary.

I have not discussed the trucking company endeavor, as it went bankrupt. Sometimes we get into things we should not. The only reason I can think of for owning the trucking business was illustrated in a conversation I had with Wilma Brown. For many years, she and her husband, Claude, owned pigs, but first they owned a very successful clothing and dry cleaning store. I asked, "Why did you own pigs?" Her response was, "We could take people out to the pigs and say, *that's my pig*." I think that explains my trucking venture, the horse racetrack, and the telephone installation business. The Brown's also lost money on their pigs. Over the years, I've developed a core competence in a few businesses. Once I stray from those areas, I lose money. Another important lesson.

I'd had a fair amount of success and some failures, but I was no longer willing to risk everything (as I had pointed out to Joe Hipple). Denise and I reviewed our finances and realized that we can live the remainder of our lives and never have to worry about money. It was time to retire. I've seen many people stay at something too long and lose everything.

Chapter 23

Ranching and Cowboys

Denise and I started the Flat Top Mountain Ranch in 1988 with the acquisition of 1,400 acres of land near Flomot, Texas. We had a cabin built next to the pond, which we stocked with bass, perch, catfish, and minnows. We have made lasting memories and shared great times there with our family and friends. Over the years we have built numerous riding trails that enable us to continually enjoy exploring the ranch on horseback. At one point, we operated nearly six thousand acres in five locations (half of the land was owned and the other half was leased) and had approximately five hundred cows. Today, we operate approximately 1,930 acres in two locations: 240 acres around our house near Muncy, Texas, and the ranch near Flomot, Texas. Our Longhorn cattle brand is the Roman numeral V. Most cattle brands have significance; ours has none. I have no idea why I chose it. (My niece Sarah said it was a divine accident—the number five in biblical numerology means *grace*—God's undeserved favor.)

The ranch land near Flomot is rich in history. The original deed for this land traces back to the JA Ranch. The JA Ranch was a partnership started by Charles Goodnight and dates to the 1870s. (It was an interesting revelation to me that this was an ancestor of Sarah Kortright, our niece who married into the family in 2007.) From 1996 to '98, an archaeological survey was conducted by students from Wichita State University. In 2004, *A Compilation of Quitaque Peaks* was published by Kathleen Dunphy as part of her requirement for a master's degree. The archaeologists assembled eighteen hundred exhibits. Among these exhibits were Indian points and hide scrapers dating back fourteen thousand years. Traces of Indian encampments were found, and, in one spot, mortar holes with depths over a foot deep were located, indicating many years of camping. On the top of Flat Top Mountain, hundreds of fragments of arrowheads have been found, several in perfect condition. Prior to the period when the land was inhabited by the Indians, the survey proved this land had been under water; examples of freshwater clamshells have been found. The artifacts that were uncovered from this period include a preserved fish fossil, a camel ulna bone, and a partial tooth from a mastodon all dating from the Triassic Period (248 to 206 million years ago).

Good ranching requires that you maintain the land. We have removed mesquite bushes and cedar trees that drain moisture out of the soil and restrict the forage of livestock and game animals. We have removed years of accumulated trash in an effort to restore the land to its natural state. We have replaced or rebuilt approximately ten miles of fence. The person responsible for this is Santos Mariscal Jr., ably assisted by our son Patrick, who worked over the summers between grade school and college. Today, three wells on the ranch are solar powered. These were installed to replace the original windmills. We have left one windmill standing near the Flat

CHAPTER 23

Top Mountain. Whenever we do anything on the ranch, we are careful not to disturb the natural beauty of the land. When someone asks if I own the land I reply, "No, the Lord owns the land, and I've been entrusted with its use for a short period of time. My task is to be a good steward."

The ranch's terrain varies from flat to mountainous, and in one area, the water from the underground aquifer can be seen in a unique way, dripping from an overhang, creating a cool, moist area where ferns, moss and other vegetation thrive. I've been told that the Indians called these the "Dripping Springs." We are happy that the local Boy Scouts enjoy camping on the ranch. A Boy Scout leader asked me why I allow the boys to camp on the ranch. I've explained that I'm paying back for the many times I was allowed to camp on someone's land when I was a Boy Scout.

At one point, we had around five hundred cows spread over six parcels of land. One place that we leased was north of Turkey, Texas, and had the distinction of being the place where Bob Wills was raised. (Bob Wills was a popular "country swing" singer in the 1940s and '50s whose signature song was "Faded Love.") Because of the size and roughness of the land, it usually took two days to gather the cattle. Denise came with us to help. On the evening of the first day, we decided to wash up in a water tank. That was quite a scene and we still laugh about it. One morning we were getting ready to gather cows; the coffee was brewing over the campfire and the cowboys were saddling their horses. I was thinking that this was right out of the Old West when, suddenly, two F16s flew over at about two hundred feet—so much for the Old West.

We leased the Bob Wills place for five years. One year we had to move the cows to my place by Flomot (i.e., the Flat Top

Mountain Ranch). We gathered most of the cows on our first day and had scheduled trucks to pick up the cows to move them by noon the next day. That morning we gathered the remainder of the cattle and had approximately 150 cows with their calves. Ty Williams noticed that one cow didn't have her calf with her. What to do? We decided that Ty would stay with the other cowboys and load the trucks, we would turn the lone mother cow loose, and I would follow the cow and see if she could find her calf. Most people think that a cow is stupid; I can tell you that isn't so. The cow left the pen and started walking with me and my horse about a quarter-mile behind. The Bob Wills Ranch is in rough country and is thick with cedar trees and mesquite bushes. The cow led me on a two-mile straight-line course to her calf. I arrived with my shirt torn and my arms full of cuts from mesquite thorns. The area where the calf had been was so thick with tall grass, I would have walked within a foot of her and never seen her. I waited while the mother cow nursed her calf, then got behind her and walked her and her calf to the pens for loading. I've seen a mother cow chase coyotes and dogs away from their calves. When I have to handle a calf, I make sure I separate it from its mother. They can be very protective, they outweigh me, and on foot they are faster. Santos saw me scale a six-foot fence in one bound and was amazed that a person of my age could be so agile. I explained, "That cow that was chasing me had three-foot horns—that was all the motivation I needed."

In 1995 we purchased a half section (320 acres) of land near Aiken, Texas. My plan was to convert the land, which had been growing row crops (cotton, wheat, etc.) into a pasture for cattle. I had read about an enriched grass from New Zealand

CHAPTER 23

that had a high yield, grew rapidly, and was well suited for cattle grazing.

The farm had two water wells on it. As there had been no need, the land was not fenced, so I hired some farm hands to install five-strand, T-post mounted barbed wire. After investigating several designs, I purchased a sprinkler system. The system was constructed on ten-foot aluminum wheeled towers and moved like a windshield wiper. The system moved at whatever speed was programmed into the computerized control. It was an impressive structure. As the field sloped to the south, the towers disappeared over the hill.

The grass was planted and watered. The first year the abundance of grass far exceeded expectations. At first, we stocked the farm with Holstein cattle, which we partnered with a local farm. The partnership began when we purchased the Flat Top Mountain. With the expansion of the Holstein herd came never-ending problems. Without going into too much depth, it seemed like a repeat of my experience with Cable Investments. I ended this partnership and purchased Angus cows. My plan was to raise the cows and develop a cow/calf operation.

We established a breeding cycle to produce a calf in mid to late March. The gestation period of a cow is nine months. The first year of operation, I arranged to have the cows artificially inseminated during late May/early June of 1997. I hired Ty Williams to do this. The delivery date was selected so that the new calves would mature during the warmest part of the year.

The winter of 1997-1998 turned out to be the coldest anyone could remember. What was accurate was the birthing of the calves. We struggled through the winter with frozen hoses and broken water lines. Santos Mariscal and I spent many days tending to the cattle. The fellow that was supposed to be doing this always seemed to be missing when times were tough.

The worst three days of that whole winter were March 15, 16, and 17—strong winds, bone-chilling temperatures, and rain mixed with sleet and snow. We gathered the cows in pens near our work area. Each day I watched the expectant mothers. Ty Williams, Santos Mariscal, Denise, and our son Patrick helped when they could. Each day, Ty would inspect the cattle and point out which cows looked like they were ready to deliver their calf. The weather fluctuated between light snow and freezing drizzle. The cows had been inseminated with semen from Chianina bulls and were known to produce large calves. As my cows had had calves in prior years, I was convinced this should not be a problem—a huge mistake.

I had observed calves being pulled and had read a book on the procedure. When a cow is having a problem delivering, you have to pull the calf. There's a device with a u-shaped bracket that fits over the cows rear end and a long handle with a "come along" attached. What's required is that you reach into the cow's uterus, locate the calf's feet, tie ropes around the feet above the first joint, attach the rope to the come along, and crank. With luck, the calf will come out without killing it or the mother. We had one hundred and fifty cows and we had to assist approximately one-third of the deliveries. The romantic image of the cowboy riding through his cows, singing, faded quickly.

One cow required a C-section—this I could not do. Our veterinarian, Bud Johnston, came over to do this during a particularly heavy downpour. When he was finished, he told Patrick and me to roll the cow so that the water would run out and he could sew her up.

CHAPTER 23

When the crisis was over and the cows looked contented, they were turned out into the pasture. The next day, my missing cowboy was checking the calves and called me. When I got to the Aiken place, we walked to the bottom of the pasture where ten calves were stuck in the mud and killed by coyotes. For those reading this and wondering why ranchers shoot coyotes—this is why. The image of the solitary hunter howling at sunset is a myth. They hunt in packs and are opportunistic killers. On one hunting expedition, I shot a coyote from the truck bouncing across the pasture. The fellow driving was an ex-marine and could not believe I made the shot.

That next year Denise, Patrick, and I were visiting my son James and his family. At a steak house in Greenwich, Connecticut, our conversation turned to ranching. I commented that the steak looked familiar. Patrick proceeded to describe in graphic detail how to pull a calf. The restaurant was crowded and Patrick was plainly heard. He described, "Daddy was pulling on the calf, and I was pulling on Daddy." He explained in vivid terms how I reached in and pulled out the afterbirth. What emptied the restaurant was his animated account of the C-section.

I've sold this land, but I will never forget the winter of 1998.

I made a practice of recording the history of each cow. One day while we were working our cows (inoculations, tagging, etc.), we divided the work; I would catch their head in the work pen and tell the recording person the cow's number. The first cow came through, I shouted out "145!" The person giving the inoculations said, "Jim, that's 451." The next cow was "302"—*oops!*—"203." Finally, we decided that I should do the inoculations. My old malady (dyslexia) had reared its ugly head.

THE NOT SO GREAT AMERICAN NOVEL

One year, Denise was in a theater group in Plainview. At the cast party, I was talking to one of the other husbands about cattle. After a few minutes the fellow said, "If you want to see some really excellent cattle, you should go over to Olton and see Kevin Igo's cattle." It was hard for me to contain myself, as I had sold Kevin those cows.

I partnered with Ty Williams on 150 cows. We purchased the cows from a ranch in New Mexico and grazed them for about six months. During that time, most of the cows had calves. We drove the cows and calves to the sale barn approximately five miles down a dirt road; it was a blast. We caught the market on a good day and received top dollar for the cows. After the sale, Ty told me that a fellow by the name of Jim had purchased the cows and that I should shake his hand.

Here is a little background. I had purchased a bank from Jim's brother. When we sold the banks to City Bank, one loan out of thousands was no good—Jim's. I felt that his brother should have made good on this, but he did not. I worked out how to purchase Jim's loan personally so that City Bank could close the purchase of the Banks—you cannot buy a bank with a known bad debt (i.e., a non-performing loan) on the books. The president of City Bank knew that the brothers had acted underhandedly. We set up an agreement that City Bank would administer Jim's loan. Each year like clockwork I received a check made out to me via City Bank from Jim. We turned the tables on him.

I had never met Jim before. Ty took me over to meet him and I grabbed his hand and said, "Jim Doucette, nice to meet you. Thank you for buying our cows." The color drained from his face as he realized that the fellow he thought he had cheated on his loan, and who had pursued him until he paid it back,

CHAPTER 23

had just made a lot of money selling him cows. I think Jim finally understood the meaning of "payback."

There has been much written about the American cowboy. I've spent many years around cowboys. One thing I've learned is that you accept them for what they are or not at all. I believe that a cowboy has a different view of the world from most folks. I'd like to tell a few stories and try to capture what I think it is to be a cowboy.

A number of years ago, a friend of mine who was raising emus realized that market price for emus had dropped to the point where it did not make sense to feed them. We came up with a solution: turn the emus loose on the ranch. After the emus had been on the ranch a few months, they wandered off. We heard stories of them traveling to Flomot, Turkey, and throughout the Quitaque Valley. A cowboy friend of mine, Shawn Williams, told me he had roped one of the emus and had loaded it in his trailer. When he put his horse in behind the emu, the horse kicked the sides out of the trailer. I asked him why he had done that. His response: "Well, it seemed like a good idea at the time."

We had been gathering cows at the Bob Wills ranch north of Turkey, Texas. Ty Williams rode up to the pens and appeared visibly shaken. I asked him what happened. As he was riding, he spotted a wild hog and thought it might be fun to rope it. As Ty tells it, he did not realize how much a hog resents being roped. After he got the rope on the hog, the hog turned around and charged the horse. The horse immediately started running away, and Ty exclaimed, "You'd be surprised how fast a wild hog can run; he almost caught the horse! That hog did not seem to tire, either." After the hog finally got tired, Ty was able to escape, minus a fifty-dollar rope. I asked him,

"Why did you rope that hog?" His response: "Well, it seemed like a good idea at the time."

I believe that a real cowboy is a person who will do almost anything so long as "it seems like a good idea at the time."

Cowboys have their own system of values. When we moved to West Texas, a day-work cowboy's pay was fifty dollars a day and he had to supply his own horse. A workday can vary. One description of it is "you work from *can*, to *can't*." No matter the length of the day the pay is the same; the cowboys accept this without complaint. But, ask a cowboy to get off his horse to walk a fence line and you will never see him again.

Denise, Me and Spoon

CHAPTER 23

Flat Top Mountain Ranch, 2000: Santos Mariscal, Randy Pyles, Patrick, Me, Denise, and Leo Bertholf

Denise and Me by the water trough

THE NOT SO GREAT AMERICAN NOVEL

Santos Mariscal and Me

Randy Pyles and me

Chapter 24

Herding and Gathering Cows

Of all of the things I've done in my life, none has given me greater pleasure than the hours I've spent on the back of a horse, working cows.

I bought my first cow after we acquired the ranch. A saying you hear in West Texas is: "There's a lot they didn't tell me when I signed on with this outfit." The same can be said about owning cattle. Over the years, I've been fortunate to be associated with outstanding cattlemen and to work with excellent cowboys—truly a dying breed.

Herding and gathering cattle are two distinct activities.

Herding

We have leased and owned many sections of land. I've now sold it, but we owned a piece of land a little over a mile from our house. Many times, we moved the cows up and down the dirt road. The first time we moved cows between our properties we loaded the cows onto trailers and drove them to the pasture by our house. When you load a cow onto a trailer, the cows become extremely agitated and develop "scours" (i.e., diarrhea), which results in a 5 to 10 percent weight loss. Cattle are sold by the pound; it's easy to calculate that moving a thousand-pound cow by trailer can cost you a lot of money. Additionally, loading and unloading cattle is dangerous work, so I decided to try herding the cows on horseback down the road. Once we did it this way, we never used the trailers again.

When you herd cows on horseback, the watch words are: "Take your time." The moves up and down the road were accomplished by Denise, Patrick, Santos, and I. We worked out a routine. Another old saying: "One cowboy can't move one cow, two can't move any, and three can move a thousand cows." We added a fourth person in front in a pick-up truck, which was also the truck we used to feed the cows.

Another cattle drive that we did was about eight miles from a pasture we leased to the sale barn in Floydada. This was a major undertaking as we had cows with new calves. Our crew consisted of John Hindman, Randy Pyles, Ty Williams, Denise, Patrick, Santos, me, and two day-work cowboys. We first had to gather the cows and let them settle and as carefully as possible, push the cows through a gate and down the dirt road towards town. We were fortunate that these cows had always been worked by cowboys on horseback. The drive started out with one cowboy in front (a cow will follow a horse). As the cows exited the pasture, they were flanked on each side by a cowboy who formed a man/horse moving wall with sufficient spacing so that if a cow decided to make a break, someone was there to push her back into the herd. At the back of the herd were a truck and trailer, and several cowboys with ropes for stragglers. These stragglers were loaded into the trailer.

What none of us knew was how the local police would react to a hundred and fifty cows with their calves being driven across Highway 70. Rather than ask for permission ahead of time, we called the Floydada Police Department when we were halfway there. To our surprise, the police were happy to block the highway and allow us to cross. It turned out to be a

CHAPTER 24

mini parade. Had we transported the cows via trailer, the cost in weight loss would have been substantial. Over the years, we had many cattle drives.

Gathering

When I refer to gathering cows, I'm talking about bringing cows together so that they can be worked (i.e., branded, given shots, separated for transport, etc.). The pastures we work on vary in nature from flat, even farm land to rough canyon land. Many times we've gathered our cows on our ranch (Flat Top Mountain).

A lot depends on the experience of the cowboys. I've spent the whole day gathering cows only to have a gate left open by accident. Our ranch land is rough and you have to constantly be one step ahead of the cows, which is sometimes harder than one would imagine.

In the fall of 2013, I helped a friend of mine, Steve McPherson, gather his cows at his ranch. The ranch is located south of Palo Duro Canyon State Park, probably one of the most picturesque canyons in the country, after the Grand Canyon. I call this next story "Catching 310." I share this story from a viewpoint in the present, as it reflects so many occasions of gathering cows on the ranch.

Catching 310

It's dark when I arise at 4:00 am. I make a "to go" cup of coffee, and head for the barn. I don't have to worry about going out to the field to get my horse as I put him in the barn the night before.

THE NOT SO GREAT AMERICAN NOVEL

It's a cool, crisp autumn day. The first thing to greet you is the smell of the earth, rich and full. This smell always reminds me of my grandfather's farm, with the clear, clean odor of mother earth.

It's a short drive to the barn. I really don't need the truck except for its lights. The drive to the barn is short but not without pleasure. The dogs are up and barking, "Take us with you!" I answer, "Sorry, not today." A rabbit scampers across the road. Arriving at the barn, I hear my horse, Spoon, moving around. He knows that today is going to be special. Catching him is easy as he is well trained. He moves around but makes no effort to run away.

After I've turned the barn lights on, I park my pick-up truck and begin to saddle him. I never rush. Each move I make I've made a hundred times before. A horse by its nature is a docile animal. Its natural reaction to anything new is to run away. This God-given instinct is what has kept the species alive. It's a prey animal and man is on top of the food chain—the number-one predator. You're asking the horse to let you ride on its back, while his very nature is telling him to run away. It takes many hours of patient, repetitive training for a horse to accept a rider.

I know my horse and he knows me. The much-rehearsed ritual of saddling is accomplished quickly and without incident, beginning with brushing the horse off where the saddle will be placed and then checking his girth (where the cinch will go) to make sure there are no burs or dirt to irritate him. I also make a quick inspection: no cuts, bumps, or bruises.

I lunge (trot in a circle) the horse and check that he is not limping. After placing the halter on the saddle horn, it's time to load him on the trailer. Loading the horse looks easy and it

CHAPTER 24

is because we've spent hours practicing. You're asking this prey animal to enter an enclosed area from which there is no escape.

It's always a pleasure to drive my Ford F-250 (my diesel ranch truck a.k.a. Big Blue) with the stock trailer as it puts me in the proper frame of mind for the task ahead. The drive to Steve McPherson's farm takes about one half hour. It's still dark, rabbits dart across the road with a sense of urgency only they know. Arriving is always a treat. I'm given a tortilla filled with refried beans. I don't need his coffee, as I have brought my own. On this trip, I'll leave my truck and trailer at Steve's and load Spoon in his trailer with his horses. The transfer is accomplished with a minimum of fuss, as his horses are also well trained.

The ride to the ranch is a pleasure. We discuss the weather, grandchildren, and cattle prices. We have our second tortilla with refried beans and arrive at the ranch in the gray hour before sunrise. A gentle mist covers the land. We drive over a cattle guard and continue about a quarter of a mile to a set of cattle pens.

The sun is beginning to rise as we unload the horses. Steve has hired three day-work cowboys, but they have not arrived. This gives me time to warm up my horse. I remember Clinton Anderson's maxim, "You have to be able to control the horse's foot movement: forward, backward and side to side." It's important to be able to flex the horse's head with light pressure on the reins; Spoon doesn't miss a cue.

The day-work cowboys arrive in a cloud of dust; they are late. One look tells me how their day began. Rising late, they rushed to the barn, chased down the horses, threw the saddles on their backs and jammed them into the trailer. It's time for me to dismount; I know what's coming. The horses fall out of the trailer, the cowboys spring into the saddle. What follows is an impromptu rodeo. As the cowboys are young and agile, they stay in the saddle, but not without incident. One of the horses manages to run through and break the reins of the horses tied to Steve's trailer, but no one is hurt. After minor repairs and saddle adjustments, we're ready to move out.

The sun is beginning to peek its head above the rim of the canyon. We proceed at a fast trot to the trail down the canyon wall, with light-hearted banter about the skill displayed during the rodeo, and who managed an eight-second ride (the time used in real rodeos to measure a successful ride).

As we begin our descent down the trail, the sun casts shadows and begins to expose the red, orange and white strata on the canyon wall, typical of this area; it's a beautiful sight. The trail is steep and narrow, and in places, the horses slide down. I maintain a safe distance from the cowboys, as I'm not certain their horses have had enough "rodeo." It takes twenty minutes to travel the mile-long trail. The horses have settled down and everyone is doing well. What is unsettled is who won this morning's rodeo.

The ranch is eight miles long, running north to south, and a mile and a half wide. There are several stream beds and numerous hills covered with mesquite and cedar bushes. The grazing is scarce this year, as we've been in a sustained drought. The soil is sandy because at one time this was an inland sea.

It takes nearly an hour to traverse the ranch at a fast trot. A couple of cowboys kick their horses into a lope (a running pace). This is not a good idea as a horse expends twice the energy running than it does at a trot. I comment that we have to ride the horses all day. I believe Steve made similar comments as they settled into a trot for the balance of the trip.

CHAPTER 24

At the fence line that ends Steve's ranch, we stop and rest the horses. The game plan for the day is discussed and everyone is given their assignment. I'm to ride the east side of the ranch with one other cowboy. This side of the ranch is not grazed often as the grass is much better on the west side, but it needs to be covered. While Steve never said it, I believe the east side is reserved for senior citizens.

We spread out down the fence line and begin our journey north, quickly losing sight of each other. My responsibility is to cover the quarter mile in front of me and to drive any cows I find to the first set of pens and water tanks. Riding through mesquite thickets can be painful as they're full of thorns. You're thankful for the chaps you wear that protect your legs because, if you're not careful, you'll have the clothes ripped right off of you.

I spot a cow with an ear tag number of 310. Spoon and I give chase. We chase it for about half an hour, managing to keep it heading north; we slide down stream banks, jump small bushes, and a mesquite thorn drives through my chaps. But this cow is ours and we are going to win the battle. Up ahead I see the pens; the other cowboys have gathered eighty cows, calves, and bulls. I look down and 310 is nowhere to be found. We back track but can't find it. I had one cow to gather and missed it.

After we've settled into position around the cows forming a man/horse wall preventing the cattle from returning to the south, Steve rides over and I relate my tale of cow 310. Steve says, "We've been chasing her for two years. You got her further than anyone else." *Little consolation.*

The cows settle down, Steve signals, and we begin pushing the cows to the next set of pens and water tanks, a distance of two miles. What starts as an orderly move, quickly turns into a battle of wills; the cows want to go south and we want them to go north.

There's an old cowboy maxim, "The slower you push cattle, the faster you get done." I know this to be true for most cattle. These are not most cattle. They are Corrientes. They descended from the cattle the Spanish brought to the New World. I've heard many translations of the word Corrientes, but the best one that describes these is "crazy cows."

We push the cows, they resist. Then three or four break for the south with cowboys after them. They are turned and return to the herd to wait for another chance to escape. I'm always surprised how agile a cow is. You'll be following them and all of a sudden, you're going across a gully and up a trail that only a mountain goat could follow. All thoughts of "cowboy cool" disappear as you seize the saddle horn and hold on for dear life.

We arrive at the second set of pens with most of the cattle we started with. It's time for a rest. After a short break, we form up for the push to the next set of pens a couple of miles away. The cows have settled down but two bulls begin to fight for breeding rights. It's nearing 10:00 am and we have to get the cows up the trail and to the pens at the top of the canyon.

The other riders exit the pen to flank the cows as they depart. My job is to make sure all of the cows leave the pen. The bulls are still fighting and I have no desire to get into the middle of it. I've seen a bull get under a horse and rider and lift them off the ground with its strong neck muscles. This happened to Denise. The winner can have his choice of the cows when we are finished with them, but right now our goal is to gather the cows and calves.

The topography to the final set of pens is not as rough as what we've been going through, a very pleasant ride aside from

CHAPTER 24

the occasional "jail break." The final push is up the trail we came down earlier and is carefully choreographed.

No more than two or three cows can climb abreast. The key is to get the first cow to make a move up the trail. All herds have an "alpha" female; get her to move and the rest will follow. My assignment is to clear all of the cows out of the final pen. My position at the rear affords me a bird's eye view of the parade up the trail. I suspect this is always reserved for the "senior citizen," as I've done it many times.

Steve knows his cows and quickly cuts out the lead (alpha) cow and encourages her up the hill while the cowboys hold the rest in place.

Once started, the ascent proceeds smoothly, except for minor rebellions. There isn't anywhere for the cows to go except up. On the way up, we have several stops at plateaus. We get a chance to look back at this beautiful country. The herd catches onto the drill and scrambles up to the next rest area. This is no time for yelling or slapping your rope; a stampede would end in disaster. Slow, steady progress is all that's required.

We arrive at our destination—the pens we started at. It's time to get off the horses, take them to water, and let them rest. After the horses are cared for, it's time for lunch—Steve has brought a cooler with sandwiches and sodas. The discussion resumes about who won this morning's rodeo; no victor is chosen. After a short rest, it's time to separate the calves from the cows; this is the last time they'll see mama.

This year I have been promoted. Usually I open and close gates, but this time I'm to assist with the sorting on horseback. As others separate the cows from their calves, it's my job to hold the calves in the alley they have been sorted into. Spoon and I have to stand off to the side as the calves are driven down the alley. After that, it's our responsibility to keep the calves from rejoining their mothers. There are only two things you have to know to work cattle: they will usually run away from you, and you have to be smarter than a cow (that's the hard part). What you try to do is have the cows run away from you to the place you want them.

The sorting process is a lot of fun. It's a pleasure to be on the back of a horse with "good cow sense." There is no way a rider can spur a horse to counter a calf's movements. They are very quick, but Spoon is quicker. That's not to say we win every battle, but after an hour, we have all the calves that are leaving sorted out of the herd.

Only two procedures remain; spraying the mother cows with Ivamec (this will keep them free of flies and ticks), and loading the calves into a trailer. The spraying is easy. One cowboy stands by the gate, while the cows are urged out. This is done slowly as you don't want a jam-up at the gate with the cows pushing and shoving. This is accomplished and the mamas are free to return to the canyon and get ready for next year's calf.

Loading four- and five-hundred-pound calves onto a truck is not a job for the faint of heart. For this task, I'm happy to be a senior citizen. The day-work cowboys are assigned this task. These calves have never seen a trailer before. It takes a combination of brute force and cattle prods to get them up the ramp and into the trailer. After watching them work, all thoughts of their being late are forgotten. These are tough kids (real cowboys).

With the day's work behind us, we load the horses for the ride home. The sun is dipping out of sight as we leave the ranch. Arriving at Steve's farm, we unload the calves. Once

CHAPTER 24

more, I wear my senior citizen's badge and don't have to go into the trailer to push the calves out. All tasks completed, we say our goodbyes until next time.

I'm tired on the drive home, but it's a good tired. The dogs bark their greeting and the rabbits scurry. At my barn-tack room, I unsaddle Spoon and brush him. We've had a good day. I say to Spoon, "Next year we'll catch 310."

Chapter 25

Non-Business Activities

We purchased land near Muncy, Texas, in 1989 as a place to pasture our horses. After Patrick was born, our house in town became crowded. In the fall of 1990, we engaged Danny Bowman and Marlon MacDonald to build a house on this site. There is much to learn watching craftsmen like Danny and Marlon work. I've known many people who call themselves carpenters—next to Danny and Marlon they are merely handymen. We moved into our new home in mid-1991 and have added to the house four times. I've kidded Denise about further additions; her only comment was "Nice kneecaps." I don't think we'll be doing any more additions. We've added a riding arena where we've taught young people how to ride a horse. The kindergarten children visit us each year to have their picture taken on a horse and it's a place to entertain family and friends (without sharing a bathroom).

In 1995 and 1996, I sponsored a Leadership Seminar at Wayland Baptist University for high school seniors. During the question and answer session after my presentation, one student asked what I was most proud of. Without hesitation

I said, "My four children." I think what was expected was a recap of some great moment in business.

One year, Jim and Tracey made presentations at the seminar and were big hits. Another year Marie came to visit and was asked by a grammar school teacher to talk to her class about being an artist. The kids and teachers talked about this for years. Many times, I've heard it said that people work hard and sacrifice for their children. I don't believe that. A person strives for themselves; it is nice to give your children a better life than you've had, but that's a byproduct.

One of my cousins told me I was making it too easy for my children, and that they should have to struggle as I did. *Nonsense.* All a parent can do is to make their lives somewhat easier; I've been happy to do it. I've tried to take some of the large rocks out of their way. In the final analysis, that's all a parent can do.

I'm proud that my children have had a better education than I had and that I was able to help them. One thing I know is that none of my children are lazy. They are also independent. A point that illustrates how James and Bernard think happened after my grandchildren were born. As each grandchild was born, I set up small trust funds for them. One day the boys sat me down and said, "No more trust fund money, Dad; we like the way we were brought up." At first, I was aggravated, but upon reflection, I am proud.

Life does come full circle. In 2009, I went on a twelve-day hike at Philmont Boy Scout Ranch with Patrick, then an Eagle Scout. Being a Boy Scout in Brooklyn, the thought of going to Philmont was only a dream. This is proof that prayers are answered. As I put on my backpack I was thinking, "Fifty

CHAPTER 25

years seems a little excessive in answering a prayer, but it was worth the wait."

When Patrick graduated valedictorian from high school, Bernard and James came to the graduation. The night of the graduation we had a party; Patrick and Bernard played guitars and it was a true joy to see. My father was a good musician. I guess they get their talent from him. Patrick went on to study history at Southern Methodist University (SMU) and graduated with honors Phi Beta Kappa. As of this writing, he is working for the Peace Corps in Costa Rica.

I am not surprised that Patrick has done so well. From a young age, he demonstrated a toughness that is not apparent when you meet him. He comes across as a gentle, good-natured young man. From age six to twelve, he studied martial arts. I thought this was a good idea because the exercise was good for him and they wore protective gear. One year, he informed us that there was going to be a tournament in Amarillo, and he was going to fight. We went to the tournament thinking, *Our little boy is going to be beat up!* When it was Patrick's turn to fight, I had my eyes partially closed. I only hoped he would not get hurt. His opponent scored first (a contact punch), earning him one point. This turned out to be the last point the opponent scored. I could not believe my eyes; Patrick's punches were accurate and devastating. He ended up winning first place in his age group. The determination he showed that day has stayed with him. I don't know how he will end up, but I'm confident that he will leave the world a little better than he found it.

I am convinced that, given a good environment, any young person can be successful, but this is not always the case. My children turned out well because of their environment and motivation. My personal story could have been different. At crucial times in my life, I had people that cared about me. I've been inspired to do something to help children who are less fortunate. I was presented with an opportunity that could positively change the lives of troubled young people.

In 1995, Bruce Ballou, a juvenile probation officer, came to visit me. He had an idea. Bruce had worked in juvenile probation for many years, and he was not happy with the recidivism of youthful law offenders (ages ten to seventeen), and wanted to do something about it. His idea was to purchase a building in Floydada that the bank had repossessed and convert it into a residential facility. His plan was to use the facility as a place to teach young people basic life skills, using concentrated class work to bring them up to their grade level and teach them self-discipline. The building is located one block off the square in Floydada, formerly a department store of five thousand square feet. He wanted to know how much money would be required to purchase the building. His plan was to have a fundraiser and apply for grants. I was impressed with the plan and Bruce's determination. To his surprise, I informed him, "If you can raise this money for the remodeling, the building will be given to you." I think he had a difficult time processing this; finally I said, "Bruce, you own the building."

It took almost a year to remodel the building. The PAC (Parent Adolescent Center) opened in May 1996. The center can accommodate twenty-four youths, male or female.

During a visit, Bruce talked to me about bringing the children to my house and letting them ride my horses. I thought this was a good idea and we scheduled a visit. The first visit consisted of fifteen children and after a short demonstration, three youths mounted horses. It did not take long to realize

CHAPTER 25

that a ten-minute demonstration was not adequate. Bruce and I thought it would be a good idea to use riding lessons as a reward for good behavior at the center. The youth progressed through different levels, based on their performance, in order to complete the program. Bruce thought, as an incentive for achieving the highest level, they would be rewarded by being allowed to take horseback riding lessons. This program evolved into two-hour lessons a week and lasted until the youth graduated from the program. I conducted this program for ten years, which coincided with my cattle operation. Denise helped with the lessons, time allowing. Several of the students (male and female) progressed to a point that they helped working cattle, branding, castrating, and giving inoculations.

Working with these children was a rewarding experience. I've heard it said, "When you give, you get back twice what you gave." This understates the reward.

You can't help but get to know the PAC children. I never asked them their offense or tried to probe personal matters. One young man told me he was in PAC because he beat up his stepfather. I asked him, "Why did you do that?" He responded, "Because he hit my mother." All I could say was that he did the right thing, but that if it happened again, to call the police. After a youth completes the PAC program, and if there are no further offenses, their criminal record is wiped clean. I heard many stories of abuse. One young girl told me she was raped by her grandfather. The only thing I could say to her was, "It wasn't your fault."

During an election campaign for county judge (a member of the Juvenile Probation Oversight Board), one of the candidates visited the PAC and had some unkind words to say about it. I queried her at a meeting where she was talking about this as her criticisms were totally out of left field. Her dismissive response was, "Victims have rights," and she wanted to know what was going on. I agree; victims do have rights. Most of the troubled youths are victims. (I suspect she was trying to find an election issue.) Fortunately, she was not elected. The superintendent for the Floydada School System complained in an article about the cost of operating the PAC and wanted it closed. In reality, the school system did not have to spend any added money to provide the offsite education. The staff at PAC could not respond; I could and I did. I wrote a letter to the editor and pointed out that the superintendent seemed to, "know the cost of everything and the value of nothing." That ended his push to close the PAC.

Recently, I stopped at an Allsup's (a gas station/grocery store) in Plainview. The clerk asked me, "How is Sam?" (one of our horses). He explained that he had riding lessons when he was in the PAC. Today he is going to Wayland Baptist University in Plainview, Texas, and working to pay his expenses. I heard that another former riding student is a pen rider in a cattle feed lot.

I made it a practice of saying a prayer on my way to pick up the children for their lessons, asking the Lord to watch over us. One morning, the radio was playing when I began my prayer and suddenly I heard a voice say, *Turn off the radio*. When you pray to the Lord, give Him your full attention.

In 2000, the priest and representative of the Knights of Columbus from the Catholic Church in Floydada approached me about having a pilgrimage from the Floydada church to our property where they would have a service honoring Mary—

CHAPTER 25

The Blessed Mother of Jesus. We thought this would be a great idea. Father Phillip mentioned that it would be nice if there was a little shrine to have the service in. Without realizing it, I had agreed to build the shrine. The shrine and the crosses that occupy the site were built by Ed Marks with Santos Mariscal's assistance. We've enjoyed many days at the shrine; it's a bit of tranquility, a great place to pray.

You never know what will result from your efforts. After the shrine was completed, Paul Schacht related a story to me. He and a friend of his stopped to visit the shrine, where they encountered a man and wife exiting. During their conversation, it turned out that the man and wife had stopped to pray that he would find a job. The fellow that was with Paul said, "I've been looking for help." With that, the fellow was offered a job and accepted it. What a great story.

The only thing I messed up on was the candle concession. Since I've retired I've lost my edge. The Knights of Columbus maintain the candles and charge two dollars a candle. If I had been thinking I would have kept the candle concession. At the end of each day I could have blown out the candles and gotten another two dollars off the same candle, I'll never know how many times I could have repeated this. I could have made a fortune!

Denise has served on the Lockney Library Board since the late 1980s. The library building was small and difficult to find. One of the first things that Denise proposed was that a sign be put on the building indicating that this was the library. It was housed in a rented building approximately 30' × 100'; the roof leaked, and it was in general disrepair.

One sad day for me was closing my office. We had purchased the old bank building from the Lockney School District in 1989 and, after extensive remodeling, moved our office into the new facility. Our staff had grown rapidly; we outgrew our first office by 1987 and moved to a larger office on 108 North Main St. By 1989 our staff had grown to ten people and by remodeling the first floor of the bank building, we had sufficient room. As we added additional businesses (C4, Performance Cable TV, Central Florida Satellite, Northwest Cable, First Alarm, and the telephone installation business), our staff had grown to seventeen. We remodeled the second floor. This office served us well through the '90s, but by 2002 was no longer needed.

Denise and I discussed the sad state of the library. She had begun to work on a fundraiser to fix up the old building. We realized that the Lockney Library Association could never raise enough money to pay for the remodeling and decided to give our office building to the library. We hired Marlon McDonald and Danny Bowman to construct the shelving and to make what adjustments were needed to accommodate it. The new library was opened in 2002. As a result of the move, utilization of the library has increased tenfold, a youth summer reading program has been established, and funds were raised to purchase three computers for public use and one for the librarian.

The Library Association purchased a bronze sculpture of a brother and sister riding a tricycle and dedicated it to me and my sister, Marilyn, who was a volunteer librarian and served on the Library Board until her death in 2005. During a visit by my Aunt Lucille Doucette, we toured the library. The li-

CHAPTER 25

brarian took a picture of us in front of the bronze sculpture. Every time I pass the library, I'm reminded of the poem "A Book" by Emily Dickinson.

> There is no Frigate like a Book
> To take us Lands away,
> Nor any Coursers like a Page
> Of prancing Poetry;
> This Traverse may the poorest take
> Without oppress of Toll,
> How frugal is the Chariot
> That bears a Human soul.

It is my hope that young people discover reading before I did. The first book I read cover to cover was *The Machinist Mates Manual* when I was in the navy. "Too soon old, too late smart."

Denise and I tithe. We keep track of everything we spend by a month-by-month financial statement. It's tough to give money to worthwhile causes; there are a lot of charlatans. We've tried to invest it in our town. We've worked on many projects: day care centers, the local hospital foundation, and youth projects ranging from scholarships to activities.

The Lord gives you back more than you give out.

I don't look for it to come back, but *it always comes back*. This has happened to me so many times that I could almost write a book about it.

Chapter 26

Church Family

My spiritual life was "kick-started" by my mother. She promised, when she married my father, that she would bring us up in the Catholic faith. When Eunice gave her word, by God, she kept it. The days I did not want to go to church, I heard her oath and felt her foot.

When Denise and I married, we could no longer receive the sacraments of the Catholic church, as I was divorced. I discussed this with a Catholic priest. He told me I could get an annulment, and my question was, "What do I tell my children?" (An annulment would have been like saying my children were 'illegitimate'.) He had no answer. This to me was a divorce with a wink—I don't wink.

After Denise and I moved to Lockney and she became pregnant, we discussed what to do about church attendance. It was important to us that our son be raised in a church and be exposed to Christian faith. We visited several churches; many required that you be re-baptized, thereby renouncing your Catholic baptism, which we would not do. I've recently read that the Catholic church is talking about letting divorced people receive communion—finally.

One day, Barry Barker invited me to visit the First United Methodist Church of Lockney (FUMC). At that time, Tommy Beck was the minister. His sermon was straightforward. His blessing at the end of the service struck me, "I hope this is the greatest day of your life because you've allowed Jesus Christ to be a part of it."

On the Sunday that communion is served (i.e., the first Sunday of each month), Tommy explained that communion in the Methodist church is "open"; anyone can receive, it is up to you to be sorry for your sins, ask forgiveness, and accept Jesus as your Lord and Savior. I knew that Don Williams attended the Methodist church in Plainview, Texas. He and I discussed the doctrines and structure of the Methodist church. Don pointed out that the church accepted everyone. He had taught Sunday school for many years and was able to answer my questions. We did not have to be re-baptized, only promise to follow the teaching of the church, which can be boiled down to two commandments: love God with all your heart, and love your neighbor as you love yourself. After thinking about the requirements to be a member of the Methodist church, Denise and I joined. I've invited many people to our church, and I explain, "The Methodist church accepts anyone. I'm living proof."

Being a member of FUMC of Lockney is not a passive act. Immediately, I was asked to join the Administrative Council, the committee that oversees the church. The church is run by the congregation and establishes the annual budget. The pastor is a member of the committee but is not its chairman. I've observed in other churches that the committees are mostly for show; they can discuss all they want but the pastor or monsignor does what he wants. The church is totally funded by the

CHAPTER 26

congregation. While I was chairman of the finance committee there was a shortfall developing in our collections. After discussing it with the committee members, it was decided that I would explain the financial problem to the congregation. I was given time during one Sunday service and outlined the problem as I saw it. Our pastor kept silent. I had no idea how this was going to be received as the farmers were having a bad year, but within two months the shortfall was covered. I had memories of a priest getting up week after week to admonish the congregation to "dig deeper" into their pockets. At FUMC Lockney, all you have to do is outline the problem. A number of years later, one of our pastors took it upon himself to scold the congregation for not contributing more. He did not realize that our money does not flow equally throughout the year as the farmers made their donations to the church after harvest. Had he asked, I would have explained it to him. After this sermon, the attitude towards him eroded and he was replaced that next year. When our new pastor arrived, I made a point to visit with him. I explained that if the church has a financial problem, the finance committee would handle it. I summarized by saying, "Your job is faith and morals—you have enough work to do."

Our church decided many years ago that we should reach out to the youth of our community. We have a lot of teachers in our congregation and a program called Kids' Time was instituted on Wednesday afternoon during the school year. This would be in addition to Vacation Bible School offered each summer. This was easy for me to agree with as we had such qualified people to handle it. Little did I know that Dani Johnson was going to ask me to help Jerry Ford do the weekly bible story. This has convinced me that the Lord has a sense of humor. It's also one of the most difficult and rewarding activities I've ever been involved with.

I've heard our congregation referred to as a "church family." This is not something you hear in New York. It takes time to accept this. While I was recovering from cancer, there was not a week that went by that I did not receive a card, a telephone call, or a visit from a member of my "church family." They were always there for me. After my niece Susan was diagnosed with breast cancer, Shawnda Foster (a church member) called me and went over the schedule of who would drive Susan to her treatments each day. She did allow that I probably wanted to continue to take Susan for treatment on Tuesdays, as that was the day she met with her doctors, but if I had a problem there were more than enough volunteers to cover for me. I never asked for help—that's just what families do.

What distinguishes one Christian church from another are practices, not theology. I'm certain that many will disagree with this statement, but this is what I believe; a church should be all-inclusive. Isn't that what Jesus taught us?

In January 2004, our church began a bible study called "Forty Days of Purpose" by Rick Warren. We discussed the composition of the small groups that would work together on a weekly basis. While we were discussing this, I asked if someone would invite my sister, Marilyn, to their group. Andy Ford volunteered and Marilyn accepted. She's my only sister, and we had been through a lot together, but I felt she'd be more comfortable with strangers.

After Marilyn's husband, George, passed away in 1983, she continued her job at a health clinic and we purchased a co-op apartment for her to live in. By 1991, I could tell that New York had little that interested her. We talked about her moving

CHAPTER 26

to Lockney, and after several visits, she relocated. It was an easy move as we had moved to our new home five miles from town and Marilyn moved into our place in town. Additionally, my daughter needed a place to live, so she moved into Marilyn's co-op apartment in Brooklyn.

My sister adjusted well to Lockney, began working in my business, and quickly made friends. She knew we attended the Methodist church. I knew she had fallen away from the Catholic church, and on rare occasions, would attend our church. To my amazement, she not only attended the weekly study but began regularly attending our church. Our church family embraced her and I sensed a contentment in my sister that had been missing.

On March 23, 2005, my sister went to the Lockney Hospital, unable to breathe. The hospital transferred her to the Lubbock Heart Hospital. I followed the ambulance. In a coma, she was admitted and placed on a respirator. She never regained consciousness. I called her daughter Susan, who was living in Arizona. She made arrangements to travel to Lubbock the next day. Later that day, her doctor told me that there was nothing to be done, and that she should be removed from the respirator and allowed to pass in peace. I asked if he could wait until her daughter arrived, to which he agreed.

The next day I picked up Susan and brought her to the hospital. When Susan entered Marilyn's room, her vital signs escalated. I'd never seen anything like this before. Susan had contacted Steven Anderson, her husband George's son, whom my sister had raised. Steven would fly into Lubbock the next day. Susan stayed with her mother that night. The next morning we again met with the doctor. It was obvious that continuing the respirator served no purpose. The doctor arranged to have the tubes removed from Marilyn at noon. He told us that she would probably pass on within fifteen minutes. We agreed to stay with her and, unfortunately, Steven was not scheduled to arrive until 3:00 pm.

With the respirator removed, we sat by my sister and waited. Around 2:30 pm I went to the airport. During the ride to the hospital, I explained the situation to Steven. We arrived around 3:30 pm, entered the room, and at Marilyn's side, I told her that Steven was there. He held her hand and her vital signs escalated as they had before.

We waited another hour and she died with her eyes wide open and a smile on her face. Her funeral was attended by my sons, our church, several of my former employees, and Marilyn's Lockney friends. Our church was full. The weather was terrible in New York, the airports closed. I have no idea how my sons, James and Bernard, and my cousin Russell Bergin, were able to get to Lockney. What fine men. The hospice care center planted a tree in her honor. Marilyn had worked as a volunteer with their patients. My mother and Marilyn were much alike.

Our church brought my sister back to her Christian faith and made her passing less painful as I know she is with the Lord. I am forever grateful to our church.

Chapter 27

Reflections

My family-of-origin's lifestyle was not consistent with a long life; most of my cousins are dead.

As I shared at the beginning of this memoir, my closest cousins were Bobby Keyes and Benny Berkowitz. In 2009, when Benny died, I was able to make it to his bedside just prior to his passing. Fortunately, my cousin Peter called to tell me of his eminent death so that I could see him one last time.

At his funeral, Benny's son, Kenny, asked me to recite a poem that is another favorite by Alfred Lord Tennyson, "Crossing the Bar."

> Sunset and evening star,
> And one clear call for me!
> And may there be no moaning of the bar,
> When I put out to sea,
> But such a tide as moving seems asleep,
> Too full for sound and foam,
> When that which drew from out the boundless deep

> Turns again home.
>
> Twilight and evening bell,
>
> And after that the dark!
>
> And may there be no sadness of farewell,
>
> When I embark;
>
> For tho' from out our bourne of
>
> Time and Place
>
> The flood may bear me far,
>
> I hope to see my Pilot face to face
>
> When I have crost the bar.

At Benny's funeral, a group of American Legion volunteers rendered Benny military honors for his service. Similar honors were held for Bobby when he died in 2003. In 2009, Ed Marks of Lockney asked if I would join the Veterans of Foreign Wars (VFW) and the American Legion, as they needed veterans to serve in the honor guard at funerals. I've tried to attend every funeral where we have been requested. The families are always appreciative. At each funeral, I'm always reminded of the Doucette four stars and all in my family who have served. The first funeral I attended as member of the honor guard, I was asked to be in the rifle squad. I said, "Happy to do it; will someone show me how to fire an M-1? Sailors never had to."

My cousins and I see humor in most things. Bobby visited in late summer of 2000. By that time he had a pacemaker/defibrillator for his heart, suffered from sugar diabetes, and had emphysema. His only comment was, "If I knew I was going to live this long, I'd have taken better care of myself."

CHAPTER 27

Denise and I visited Benny after he had moved to southern New Jersey, prior to his death. I accompanied Benny to the beer distributor, where he bought two cases of beer. The girl cashier carried both cases to his car, to which he exclaimed, "Girl of my dreams, where have you been all my life? A woman that can carry two cases of beer must be perfect." To this I added, "If she would knock out a few front teeth and dip snuff, she would indeed be perfect."

My cousin, Steven Berkowitz, died of AIDS in 1996. Prior to this, like many, I joked about AIDS; I no longer see any humor in this terrible disease. He was a gentle soul, who lived a conflicted life. Fortunately, Steven visited Denise and me prior to his death. We spent many days at the ranch recounting our youth.

At Benny's funeral, Peter Berkowitz asked, "Do you have any regrets?" referring to how Benny and I grew apart over the years. I responded, "I wish things had been different." What I meant was, I wish all my cousins were still with us.

Another of my mother's favorite poems was "Rock Me to Sleep" by Elizabeth Akers Allen. This excerpt sums up how I felt at the time.

> Backward, turn backward, O Time, in your flight,
> Make me a child again just for to-night!
> Mother, come back from the echoless shore,
> Take me again to your heart as of yore;
> Kiss from my forehead the furrows of care,
> Smooth the few silver threads out of my hair;
> Over my slumbers your loving watch keep;
> Rock me to sleep, mother, rock me to sleep!

In the mid-1970s my mother became disabled; her backbone disintegrated as a result of a spinal fusion (TB of the spine) when she was a young woman. On every other Saturday, I'd go visit her and clean the kitchen floor, dust, and help her as best I could. In retrospect, these were our best days; no alcohol, just quiet conversations interposed by her reading (reciting) her favorite poems. My mother memorized *The Gettysburg Address* and would occasionally recite it.

Many people view death as an end. While I'm sad at someone's passing, I know we'll be together again in heaven.

Chapter 28

What I Live For

I find it a coincidence that the address of the apartment building where my mother, sister, and I lived for many years was 786 Madison Street; today I live on FM 786. I've lost a fair amount of money playing these numbers in Las Vegas; coincidence does not pay.

I started writing as a form of therapy. It has turned into a journey—my journey. Each person has their story to tell, this is mine. My hope is that my grandchildren Matthew, James III, Brendan and Janey, and those after them, will someday read this and find something of value. My children James, Bernard, Marie, and Patrick have heard these stories so often that all I have to do is say the first few lines and they finish the story. I regret that I do not know my ancestors' narratives, except for some surface facts.

I have always had trouble relating to the younger generations, I'm not a baby-boomer. During the '60s I barely noticed the flower children, and the "Me" generation of the 1980s and '90s befuddles me. My generation was named the "Silent Generation"—our claim to fame is that we knew the "Greatest

Generation." I'm optimistic for my grandchildren as they are fine people from caring families.

My concern is for all of the single-parent children and children born into drug-infested homes, and the growing divide between the haves and have-nots. I was able to lift myself out of poverty. I had a chance to go to college; today advanced education is reserved for the rich. There isn't even vocational education to speak of; the crafts of the twentieth century have been replaced by robots. I fear that people of today's generation who are growing up as I did will be relegated to serving the privileged few. My hope is that this is a short-term aberration and our country will return to being "The Shining City on a Hill" with opportunity for all who are willing to work for it.

Much to my surprise, I was named Lockney's Citizen of the Year in 1993. I was not at the award dinner as I was out of town. Don Williams was asked to make a few comments about me. Since I was not present I'll have to paraphrase his comments. He said that, "Jim has the ability to take any problem and come to the best possible solution." I have learned the best possible solution is not always the perfect solution. My advice is to deal with the facts you have and come to the best possible answer. There will always be setbacks and disappointments, but never lose faith in yourself.

All of my life lessons can be summed up in the poem "What I Live For" by George Linnaeus Banks.

> I live for those who love me,
> Whose hearts are kind and true,
> For heaven that smiles above me,
> And waits my spirit, too;

CHAPTER 28

For all the ties that bind me,
For all the tasks assigned me,
And bright hopes left behind me,
And good that I can do.
I live to learn their story
Who've suffered for my sake,
To emulate their glory,
And follow in their wake;
Bards, patriots, martyrs, sages,
The noble of all ages,
Whose deeds crown history's pages,
And Time's great volume make.
I live to hold communion
With all that is divine,
To feel there is a union
'Twixt Nature's heart and mine;
To profit by affliction,
Reap truths from fields of fiction,
And, wiser from conviction,
Fulfill each grand design.
I live to hail that season,
By gifted minds foretold,
When men shall rule by reason,
And not alone by gold;
When man to man united,

> And every wrong thing righted,
>
> The whole world shall be lighted
>
> As Eden was of old.
>
> I live for those who love me,
>
> Whose hearts are kind and true,
>
> For heaven that smiles above me,
>
> And waits my spirit too;
>
> For the cause that lacks assistance,
>
> For the wrong that needs resistance,
>
> For the future in the distance,
>
> And the good that I can do.

The message of this poem is simple and straightforward. We spend our lives worrying about triviality when what is important passes us by. What we should focus on is easily summarized in First Corinthians 13; "Love is patient, love is kind. It does not envy, it does not boast, it is not proud, it is not self-seeking, it is not easily angered, it keeps no record of wrong. Love does not delight in evil but rejoices with the truth. It always protects, always trusts, always hopes, always perseveres. Love never fails."

Finally, to quote Forrest Gump, "… that's all I have to say about that!"

CHAPTER 28

Doucette Family, Yellowstone, 2010 (From left to right: James, Janey, Tracey, Me, Denise, Ann Marie, Brendan, Marie, James III, Bernard, Matthew, and Patrick)

Acknowledgments

It's not possible to list everyone who helped me write this, but there are several who stand out. First, my wife, Denise, who corrected my spelling and helped me remember. Second was Sarah Kortright, who corrected my grammar and sentence structure. Jeri Hawkins inspired me. My son Patrick, did an in-depth edit. My oldest son Jim, for his corrections and comments. My son Bernard encouraged me. My two best friends, Don Williams and Randy Pyles, read an early draft and helped fill in major blind spots. My mother-in-law, Alice Bertholf, and my cousin, Leah Horn, provided insights that only they could.

About the Author

James E. Doucette, Sr. was raised in Brooklyn, NY. He began his cable television career in the 1960s working for such companies as Adelphia, Warner Communications, TelePrompTer Corporation, and Cablevision Industries. In 1985 Jim acquired his own cable television systems in West Texas. A few years later he purchased five banks and several other businesses. By 1998, he had sold all of the businesses and retired.

While living in West Texas, Jim purchased some ranch land where he enjoys managing cattle and riding horses. He is a member of Rotary (a Paul Harris Fellow), the First United Methodist Church, and spends time volunteering in his community.

He has three sons, one daughter, and four grandchildren.

This book was started while he was undergoing chemotherapy and radiation treatments for cancer, and was written for his grandchildren.

Made in the USA
Charleston, SC
10 July 2015